Lucretius   *The Way Things Are*

LUCRETIUS *The Way Things Are*

The *De Rerum Natura* of Titus Lucretius Carus
translated by ROLFE HUMPHRIES

INTRODUCTION BY BURTON FELDMAN
NOTES BY GEORGE K. STRODACH

London
INDIANA UNIVERSITY PRESS
Bloomington

First Midland Book edition 1969

FOURTH PRINTING 1974

Published in Canada by Fitzhenry & Whiteside Limited, Scarborough, Ontario

Library of Congress catalog card number: 68-27349

Manufactured in the United States of America

cl. ISBN 0-253-14925-8   pa. ISBN 0-253-20125-X

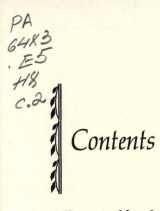

Contents

Foreword

Lucretius might, just possibly, have been born in the same year as Julius Caesar, and probably died a decade before him. His *floruit*, therefore, was in the later years of the Roman republic, well on its way to empire, world dominion, and power—to tremendous, if unevenly distributed, material prosperity. There is little evidence that the City was teeming with philosophers. It might be neat, and it might be fallacious, to conclude that materialist theory was evolved to complement and to justify materialist practice. God's way to man were not a very serious concern; there was some perfunctory observation of the homelier ancient rituals, and a good deal more excited interest in orgiastic importations from the East. There is little evidence that the men of Lucretius' time were as monstrously appalled by the fear of death as he insists; I suggest that he may have projected upon his contemporaries a terror personal to himself. Somewhere, somehow, he came upon Epicurus and his doctrines, and out of that discovery composed the great, passionate, didactic poem he called *De Rerum Natura, Concerning the Nature of Things*. For myself, I'd translate: *The Way Things Are*—simple, forthright, insistent, peremptory.

Didactic? The word gives us some trouble; we too often make it connote *preach* rather than *teach*. Lucretius, to be sure, is both teacher and prophet, but his own major emphasis stresses the teaching, the instruction, the absolute need to learn. The appeal is addressed primarily to the intellect; the power of the appeal transcends the intent, lifts to passionate emotion, becomes high poetry. None in the world higher, none more gloriously sustained.

The translator is dazzled, at the same time that he is tempted, by the highest passages, the invocation to Venus at the beginning of the poem, the last hundred or so verses of Book III, the praise of the absolute and active serenity of the gods in Book V, to cite only three of the most spectacular instances. For me, either alone or with the collaboration of some of my classes, here was the beginning. And also, for a long time, the end; suggestions that I try the entire poem, even impulses to do so, met the implacable fact that I knew all too little about modern atomic theory. A reasonable, proper, and modest diffidence, I told myself; but diffidence can be a morbid, as well as a healthy state, and some cartographers have labeled the Belgium, Gaul, and Aquitania of that province Ignorance, Laziness, Coward-ice. These qualities, my spiritual diagnosticians have assured me, are not entirely irreversible; and my retirement might just as well be conducive to recklessness as to torpor. So, finally, here we go; and somewhere along the line it crosses my mind that Lucretius knew little of modern physics either. To be sure, he had more informa-tion about atoms than I had, and some of it was even accurate. I began to find him less formidable, or myself more foolhardy, than I had anticipated; his twenty-six proofs of the mortality of the soul seemed to me less than impeccable as logic, and some of his theories of, say, images or magnetism, ridiculous. His science is, in more than one sense of the word, curious; his presentation of Epicurus' atomic theory is, in the light (or darkness) of our own time's pre-occupation, arresting. But we owe our respect and admiration not to the scientist, but to the major poet.

What gives this poem its major quality? The grandeur of the theme, to be sure, and the instructive enterprise; the scope; above all else, the tone—that wonderful high sustained peremptory aristo-cratic address to Memmius and to ourselves. It is a tone that pervades, somehow, even the areas of versified philosophy, so that this terrain is less arid and barren, more rich and illumined, than our expecta-tions might have led us to believe. It is a tone which lifts the poem beyond paradox into transcendence, beyond logic into lyric. The attack on religion becomes praise of those forces beyond the reach of Man. This *Te Deum* hymns the life-giving creativity of the power of love, the active serenity (not the Nirvana) of divine essence. Yet with all the affirmation of life, we are confronted with the attraction of death. Can Lucretius really have meant the poem to end with the horrors of the plague at Athens?

This quality of tone, both lofty and sustained, is the value I have most tried to preserve. To say it is an all-pervasive tone is not to deny that Lucretius has more than one manner. These, too, I have tried to convey, though not always in the exact same places as the poet. It is by no means easy to recognize, let alone reproduce, passages where your poet, in the original, goes in for, say, a spectacular archaicism; it is a convenient device, however, for the translator to give time this kind of twist by the use of an anachronism, even a solecism. I know perfectly well, for example, that Lucretius never saw a roll of barbed wire in his life; he may have heard Roman slang comparable to *southpaw* to describe a left-handed man. He complains of the poverty of Latin terminology to render Greek terms, but is himself by no means finicky in search for *le mot juste*, nor always consistent in particular detail. Not only nicety but also prosody determines his epithet. I have been trying to translate a poem, not to establish a one-to-one correspondence with its words.

I have followed the text of the Loeb Classical Library, as much from convenience and consistency with our practice in other translations as from devout conviction. Emendations suggested by Housman have held my gaze longer than some others, but I claim no consistency in regard to their use. I owe thanks to the editors of *The Classical Journal, The Colorado Review, The Denver Quarterly,* and *The Malahat Review* for permission to use passages which have previously appeared in their pages. In his fine book on Epicurus, Professor George Strodach of the Department of Philosophy at Lafayette College made a remark (p. 99) as immediately provocative as any argument I heard before I got down to work: "The translator of Lucretius should himself be a poet." He has contributed to this book the Synopses and Notes, and his detailed commentary on the penultimate version of the text saved me many a foolishness. He had the happy faculty of suggesting revisions which not only made more correct sense, but also were phrased in proper meter and without damage to the sonority of the line. He should not be held accountable for some pigheaded brashnesses in which I persisted. To *The Denver Quarterly* I am also indebted for the privilege of using as Introduction the unconventional and brilliant essay by Professor Burton Feldman of the English Department at the University of Denver. Finally, I must thank many collaborators, all up and down the line, at the Indiana University Press.

Rolfe Humphries

October, 1967

Introduction

All one has to do is remind oneself that it exists, to see what a puzzling poem Lucretius wrote. An important work, an undeniably great work—but the immediate problem is to remember it is there at all. It is the least visible of the great poems, even when we finally turn to look at it. What almost every lyric poem has found to praise, Lucretius' poem scorns, including the lyric mind itself—though he himself is often greatly lyrical. Pope was didactic at length, and so was Lucretius, but that doesn't help, either. In his ambitions, range, intellectual grandeur, Lucretius is much closer to the supreme epic poems, the *Iliad* or *Paradise Lost* or *Faust*. That explains something about Lucretius, but not everything, and perhaps not even what is important. For Lucretius, the epic itself is too small; he wants nothing less than to say—in one poem—everything worth saying. Like the epic poets, he wants to say something about everything and tie it all together; but with a passion for philosophy that epic poets avoid, Lucretius also wants to explain everything systematically. In doing so, he literally makes the stones speak: from indestructible atoms, all has been created and all can be explained—in one great arc, his poem moves from the atoms to mind, to sex, to the birth and growth of the world and society and religion, and ends with a coldly courageous and rational dissection of terror and death. The size of his ambition alone—not to speak of his achievement—should have kept his poem in sight. Outside of classicists and students, however, Lucretius surely has few readers. Everyone seems indifferent, but no one quite knows why. There is an uneasy feeling that perhaps it isn't a poem at all, but only philosophy versified; that the ideas are even more antiquarian than Homer's gods or Dante's Thomism; or more fatally, that it is indeed poetry; but merely dignified and second-rate. A list of our troubles with Lucretius' poem is beside the point, nevertheless, for nothing can be decided by the general reader until he can read the poem as if it were alive. There has been no good English translation of Lucretius, which raises the question—why not? Homer and Virgil have not lacked Lattimores or Lewises; why hasn't Lucretius found his English voice? A new translation can draw attention to the poem, but not necessarily keep it there. For that, the audience has to be ready for the poem. The fact that a modern poet of reputation is translating Lucretius as a poem and not as an exercise or intellectual document may be one sign that this is happening at last.

If Lucretius finally comes into his own today as a poet, it will not be for reasons often given in reviving him, convincing no one: his scientific interests anticipating ours, his materialism, or his version of the war between science and religion. That attracted a Hobbes or Gassendi in the seventeenth century, but it is not likely to matter to a modern reader, though perhaps it should. Only critics who have missed a major fact about modern poetry would present Lucretius so simple-mindedly. What should be said is that Lucretius' conception of poetry—and not his conception of science—is what nowadays may rescue his poem from neglect. However close Lucretius may be to the modern atomists, he is more rightly compared to the Eliot of the Four Quartets, to the Yeats of the *Vision*, or the Rilke of the Duino Elegies or Sonnets to Orpheus, or to the fountainheads of such modern philosophical poems about man and nature, Wordsworth's Prelude and Blake's Prophetic Books. Lucretius' poem is the first of a kind which has drawn some of the most important modern poets—an epic, not of men in passion and action, but of mind, meditation and intellectual search. Intelligence becomes its own hero; story and actor vanish as surely as Hector and Troy. The poet's mind becomes the organizing pole of experience, the only and necessary one.

Lucretius' hero is a mental hero, but—with Blake or Rilke in mind—a most unlikely one: the philosopher Epicurus, who was both a materialist and severe systematizer. Blake had his own system, but hated materialism; Rilke was inspired by matter, but had no more system than his ecstasies allowed him. It should put no reader off that Lucretius names his philosopher and follows him strictly; perhaps modern poets do not name their philosophers because they do not know who they are. It would be another mistake to think that by adopting Epicurus, Lucretius murdered his own poetic thought. On the contrary, it is Epicurus who leads Lucretius closer to us. Epicurus, says Lucretius, by the lively force of his mind "broke through the fiery walls of the world, and in mind and spirit traversed the boundless whole of things." His image is exact: a solid wall keeps one inside it, and a fiery wall majestically keeps one in fear of approaching it. These walls—of the heavens, of society, of faith in eternity or salvation—are not real, says Lucretius, and the fire is only superstitious fear. Lucretius is thus startlingly unlike Homer or Virgil or Milton—or Hölderlin or Eliot: piety, no matter how high-minded, is an illusion and intellectual disgrace that must be broken through; one must learn to live freely and unafraid in the radically open universe, in the radically unwalled truth. Whether Epicurus was right is another question. Certainly atomism and materialism are hardly the assumptions badly chosen by modern poets; but the audacious ambition is the same on both sides. The great romantic and post-romantic poets—that oddly united band from Blake and Wordsworth to Baudelaire, Rimbaud and Rilke and Yeats—moved daringly inward, through the fiery and frightening walls of accepted views about the self and soul, penetrating the authorized limits of reason, of human nature, fancy, decorum and feeling. It is also true that there are obvious important differences between the later poets and the earlier: Lucretius' great word is reason, theirs is imagination. Lucretius is driving towards a system of objects he can then use to undeceive his world and his own thought; the moderns hope to find or make a myth their world and thought can feed on. Lucretius is a poet who maneuvers by analysis and logic; the moderns are personal, improvisatory, ecstatic, inventors of new logics.

The differences are there, but they are not always to Lucretius' disadvantage. In daring boldly to strip the world of its surfaces, of its legends, limits and protections, Lucretius anticipates the urging of Yeats to go beneath the poetc embroidery concealing the naked heart of things. Put this way, the temptation may be to condescend again to Lucretius, to see him now not as an early, odd enthusiast of science, but as an early and odd enthusiast of freedom and creativity in our style. He is more or less than this. His poem shows that he is in no way to be considered less daring than his modern kin. If anything, he is often bolder. Modern poetry—in its most famous appearances—is obsessed with religion, in love with myth, mystery and wonder, often for their own sake. In one of his ways, Lucretius is that arch-enemy of the modern imagination, the rationally convinced atheist (it isn't the atheism that hurts, it's the rationality). The courage to dare—surely no one has the courage to deny that central article of our artistic faith. How refuse admiration then to a poet who attacks myth, denies the mysteries, and who—himself a poet of genius —seeks to unmask even his own poetry? If modern poets are bold enough to think that art can and should replace religion, Lucretius more boldly suggests that faith in any guise should be left unreplaced, even if it leaves a vacuum. A vision of nature undefiled and enduring has inspired modern poets to attack society and all its evil ways; and a certainty of the wholeness and livingness of nature has excited hopes that the same is true of the human soul. Lucretius dissolves the fabric and root of nature itself, ruthlessly pushing all aside as he seeks the ultimate realities in the atoms; and he is quite aware that once done, he must recognize that the heavens and world and soul are not immortal. It is poetry without illusions: sober and manly, a Roman poem republican in its modesty and imperial in its domains and claims. It is poetry without illusions, seeking only the consolations that the discursive intellect can give. The romantics, beset by science, tried to distinguish between the literature of knowledge and power: one discursively explains, the other moves. Poets in one camp shouldn't really be found fraternizing in the other camp, but Lucretius lives legitimately on both sides—and he may be the only poet who does.

So Lucretius' poem is out of joint on both ends of its history. He speaks more radically than most of the classics and Christians, but it isn't our kind of radicalism. Compared to the excitement and wonders found in the great epics and plays and novels, Lucretius seems dry: nowhere is there a hero or a battle or love or a quest tangled up in gods or grace, nothing but the philosopher's ardor of reason; nowhere a magnificently realized character of magnificence, Odysseus or Satan—nothing but the poet's voice speaking fervently of that unlikely object of poetic love, Epicurus' thoughts. Nowhere either is the poet present as Dante is, moving dramatically among the dramatic dead. Nowhere indeed is there any drama at all, as exploited by all the great poems from the *Odyssey* to *Ulysses*. Contemptuous of excitement, passion, legend and story, tradition and glory, faith and consolations, nourishing itself only on the necessities of the atoms and their occasional swervings, the poet's mind directly and nakedly seeks the truth of things. His poetry is what modern poetry often hopes it is—a search after the truth whatever the cost and knowing it will cost—poetry become genuinely philosophical. But it does not make Lucretius sit very comfortably with Blake, Rilke, or Yeats any more than with Homer, Virgil or Milton. Lucretius followed the Epicurean system, not as a mere myth or personal vision, but as the truth; but all modern poets are suspicious of philosophers and especially of systems: everyone knows about Hegel. It might seem in our time that one can be poetically philosophic (or vice-versa) without spending as much time on philosophy as on poetry. At least, all the evidence has seemed that way: for where is the poet who did not destroy his poetry by too much philosophy—look at poor Coleridge! Lucretius is the example to the contrary. His poem raises up ghosts: perhaps Coleridge was not really ruined by philosophy, but just by the wrong philosophy? Perhaps, in short, romanticism and intuition are not adequate if one would be that creature who seduces us today, the philosophical poet. Perhaps even poets should study. And modern poets especially, because the philosophic poem is often supposed to be something only a modern poet could manage: Coleridge himself said that "whatever in Lucretius is poetry is not philosophical, whatever is philosophical is not poetry; and in the very pride of confident hope I looked forward to the *Recluse* (of Wordsworth) as the first and only true philosophical poem in existence." Whether he was right or not about Wordsworth, Coleridge was wrong about Lucretius. But the fact that only Lucretius could be found as a predecessor should lead us back to his poem.

Our own dilemma and efforts may thus serve to make us read Lucretius now. Certainly, some answer to the puzzles of Lucretius' poetry can be given by a translation which rebreathes life into the poem. If Mr. Humphries has made Lucretius' language burn and bother the reader, he will have brought a great poet out of unworthy dimness. Since the truism is that form and content are indissoluble, it will be interesting to watch Lucretius dissolve them, even as we are sure it cannot be done without ruining the poetry. In the same way, he makes pain immediate and touching then dissolves it before our eyes as delusory. With the modern poet and reader in view, Lucretius may well be the most shocking and salutary poet one could find. Where could one find lines more unnerving than these:

> Our terrors and our darknesses of mind
> Must be dispelled, then, not by sunshine's rays,
> Not by those shining arrows of the light,
> But by insight into nature, and a scheme
> Of systematic contemplation.

One betrays Lucretius—and much else—if, after having read this, one blurs that "systematic contemplation" into anything more personal, visionary, or consoling than Lucretius means it. It is a lesson about poetry one can find in no other poet.

Burton Feldman

University of Denver

Lucretius   *The Way Things Are*

The line numbers at the top of each text page and in the Notes at the back of the book are consonant with those used in the Loeb edition of the poem.

Book I

Creatress, mother of the Roman line,
Dear Venus, joy of earth and joy of heaven,
All things that live below that heraldry
Of star and planet, whose processional
Moves ever slow and solemn over us,
All things conceived, all things that face the light
In their bright visit, the grain-bearing fields,
The marinered oceans, where the wind and cloud
Are quiet in your presence—all proclaim
Your gift, without which they are nothingness.
For you that sweet artificer, the earth,
Submits her flowers, and for you the deep
Of ocean smiles, and the calm heaven shines
With shoreless light.

               Ah, goddess, when the spring
Makes clear its daytime, and a warmer wind
Stirs from the west, a procreative air,
High in the sky the happy-hearted birds,
Responsive to your coming, call and cry,
The cattle, tame no longer, swim across
The rush of river-torrents, or skip and bound
In joyous meadows; where your brightness leads,
They follow, gladly taken in the drive,
The urge, of love to come. So, on you move
Over the seas and mountains, over streams
Whose ways are fierce, over the greening leas,
Over the leafy tenements of birds,
So moving that in all the ardor burns
For generation and their kind's increase,

Since you alone control the way things are.
Since without you no thing has ever come
Into the radiant boundaries of light,
Since without you nothing is ever glad,
And nothing ever lovable, I need,
I need you with me, goddess, in the poem
I try to write here, on *The Way Things Are*.
This book will be for Memmius, a man
Your blessing has endowed with excellence
All ways, and always. Therefore, all the more,
Give to our book a radiance, a grace,
Brightness and candor; over land and sea,
Meanwhile, to soldiery's fierce duty bring
A slumber, an implacable repose—
Since you alone can help with tranquil peace
The human race, and Mars, the governor
Of war's fierce duty, more than once has come,
Gentled by love's eternal wound, to you,
Forgetful of his office, head bent back,
No more the roughneck, gazing up at you,
Gazing and gaping, all agog for love,
His every breath dependent on your lips.
Ah, goddess, pour yourself around him, bend
With all your body's holiness, above
His supine meekness, drown him in persuasion,
Imploring, for the Romans, blessed peace.
For this is something that I cannot do
With mind untroubled, in this troubled time,
Nor can a son of Memmius' noble house
Falter at such a crisis, or betray
The common weal.

                     For what ensues, my friend,
Listen with ears attentive and a mind
Cleared of anxiety; hear the reasoned truth
And do not without understanding treat
My gifts with scorn, my gifts, disposed for you

With loyal industry. I shall begin
With a discussion of the scheme of things
As it regards the heaven and powers above,
Then I shall state the origin of things,
The seeds from which nature creates all things,
Bids them increase and multiply; in turn,
How she resolves them to their elements
After their course is run. These things we call
Matter, the life-motes, or the seeds of things,
(If we must find, in schools, a name for them),
Firstlings, we well might say, since every thing
Follows from these beginnings.

When human life, all too conspicuous,
Lay foully grovelling on earth, weighed down
By grim Religion looming from the skies,
Horribly threatening mortal men, a man,
A Greek, first raised his mortal eyes
Bravely against this menace. No report
Of gods, no lightning-flash, no thunder-peal
Made this man cower, but drove him all the more
With passionate manliness of mind and will
To be the first to spring the tight-barred gates
Of Nature's hold asunder. So his force,
His vital force of mind, a conqueror
Beyond the flaming ramparts of the world
Explored the vast immensities of space
With wit and wisdom, and came back to us
Triumphant, bringing news of what can be
And what cannot, limits and boundaries,
The borderline, the bench mark, set forever.
Religion, so, is trampled underfoot,
And by his victory we reach the stars.

I fear that, in these matters, you may think
You're entering upon a path of crime,
The A B C's of godlessness. Not so.

The opposite is true. Too many times
Religion mothers crime and wickedness.
Recall how once at Aulis, when the Greeks,
Those chosen peers, the very first of men,
Defiled, with a girl's blood, the altar-stone
Sacred to Artemis. The princess stood
Wearing the sacred fillets or a veil,
And sensed but could not see the king her father,
Agamemnon, standing sorrowful
Beside the altar, and the priests near-by
Hiding the knife-blade, and the folk in tears
At what they saw. She knelt, she spoke no word,
She was afraid, poor thing. Much good it did her
At such a time to have been the very first
To give the king that other title, *Father!*
Raised by men's hands and trembling she was led
Toward the altar, not to join in song
After the ritual of sacrifice
To the bright god of marriage. No; she fell
A victim by the sacrificing stroke
Her father gave, to shed her virgin blood—
Not the way virgins shed it—but in death,
To bring the fleet a happy exodus!
A mighty counselor, Religion stood
With all that power for wickedness.

                              You may,
Yourself, some time or other, feel like turning
Away from my instruction, terrified
By priestly rant. How many fantasies
They can invent to overturn your sense
Of logic, muddle your estates by fear!
And rightly so, for if we ever saw
A limit to our troubles, we'd be strong,
Resisters of religion, rant and cant,
But as things are, we have no chance at all
With all their everlasting punishments
Waiting us after death.

                    We do not know
The nature of the soul: is it something born
By, of, and for itself? Does it find its way
Into our selves when we are being born,
To die when we do? Or does it, after our death,
Tour Hell's tremendous emptiness and shadow?
Or does it, by divine commandment, find
Abode in lower beasts, as we are told
By Roman Ennius, the first of us
Chapleted with the green of Helicon,
Bright-shining through the realms of Italy?
But still, he also tells us, in his verse,
Immortal as it is, that Acheron
Has reaches where no souls or bodies dwell,
But only phantoms, pale in wondrous wise,
And that from there immortal Homer's image
(So Ennius says) transferred itself to him,
And wept, and talked about all kinds of things.
So, we had better have some principle
In our discussion of celestial ways,
Under what system both the sun and moon
Wheel in their courses, and what impulse moves
Events on earth; and, more than that, we must
See that our principle is shrewd and sound
When we consider what the spirit is,
Wherein the nature of the mind consists,
What fantasy it is that strikes our wits
With terror in our waking hours or sickness
Or in sleep's sepulcher, so that we see,
Or think we do, and hear, most audible,
Those whose dead bones earth holds in her enfolding.

I am well aware how very hard it is
To bring to light by means of Latin verse
The dark discoveries of the Greeks. I know
New terms must be invented, since our tongue
Is poor, and this material is new.
But I'm persuaded by your excellence

And by our friendship's dear expectancy
To suffer any toil, to keep my watch
Through the still nights, seeking the words, the song
Whereby to bring your mind that splendid light
By which you can see darkly hidden things.
Our terrors and our darknesses of mind
Must be dispelled, not by the sunshine's rays,
Not by those shining arrows of the light,
But by insight into nature, and a scheme
Of systematic contemplation. So
Our starting-point shall be this principle:
Nothing at all is ever born from nothing
By the gods' will. Ah, but men's minds are frightened
Because they see, on earth and in the heaven,
Many events whose causes are to them
Impossible to fix; so, they suppose,
The gods' will is the reason. As for us,
Once we have seen that *Nothing comes from nothing,*
We shall perceive with greater clarity
What we are looking for, whence each thing comes,
How things are caused, and no "gods' will" about it.

Now, if things come from nothing, all things could
Produce all kinds of things; nothing would need
Seed of its own. Men would burst out of the sea,
And fish and birds from earth, and, wild or tame,
All kinds of beasts, of dubious origin,
Inhabit deserts and the greener fields,
Nor would the same trees bear, in constancy,
The same fruit always, but, as like as not,
Oranges would appear on apple-boughs.
If things were not produced after their kind,
Each from its own determined particles,
How could we trace the substance to the source?
But now, since all created things have come
From their own definite kinds of seed, they move
From their beginnings toward the shores of light
Out of their primal motes. Impossible

That all things issue everywhence; each kind
Of substance has its own inherent power,
Its own capacity. Does not the rose
Blossom in spring, the wheat come ripe in summer,
The grape burst forth at autumn's urge? There must be
A proper meeting of their seeds in time
For us to see them at maturity
Grown by their season's favor, living earth
Bringing them safely to the shores of light.
But if they came from nothing, they might spring
To birth at any unpropitious time,—
Who could predict?—since there would be no seeds
Whose charatcer rules out untimely union.
Thirdly, if things could come from nothing, time
Would not be of the essence, for their growth,
Their ripening to full maturity.
Babies would be young men, in the blink of an eye,
And full-grown forests come leaping out from the ground.
Ridiculous! We know that all things grow
Little by little, as indeed they must
From their essential nature.

A further point—
At certain times of year earth needs the rain
For happy harvest, and both beasts and men
Need nature's bounty for their lives' increase,
A mutual dependence, of the sort
That words need letters for. Do not believe
In any world without its A B C's.
Moreover, why could nature not bring forth
Men huge enough to wade the deepest oceans,
Split mountains with their hands, and outlive time?
The answer is, that limits have been set
Fixing the bounds of all material,
Its character, its growth. And, finally,
Since we observe that cultivated soil
Excels untended land, gives better yield,
It must be obvious that earth contains

Life-giving particles we bring to birth
In breaking clods, in turning surface under,
If there were no such particles, our toil
Would be ridiculous, for things would grow
Better and better of their own accord,
But—*nothing comes from nothing.* This we must
Acknowledge, all things have to have the seed
Which gives them impulse toward the gentle air.

Our second axiom is this, that nature
Resolves each object to its basic atoms
But does not ever utterly destroy it.
If anything could perish absolutely,
It might be suddenly taken from our sight,
There would be no need of any force to smash it,
Disrupt and shatter all its fastenings,
But as it is, since everything coheres
Because of its eternal seed, its essence,
Until some force is strong enough to break it
By violent impact, or to penetrate
Its void interstices, and so dissolve it,
Nature permits no visible destruction
Of anything.

                    Besides, if time destroys
Completely what it banishes from sight
With the procession of the passing years,
Out of what source does Venus bring again
The race of animals, each after its kind,
To the light of life? and how, being restored,
Is each thing fed, sustained and given increase
By our miraculous contriving earth?
And what supplies the seas, the native springs,
The far-off rivers? And what feeds the stars?
By rights, if things can perish, infinite time
And ages past should have consumed them all,
But if, throughout this history, there have been
Renewals, and the sum of things can stay,

Beyond all doubt, there must be things possessed
Of an immortal essence. Nothing can
Disintegrate entirely into nothing.

An indiscriminate common violence
Would finish everything, except for this—
Matter is indestructible; it holds
All things together, though the fastenings
Vary in tightness. Otherwise, a touch,
The merest touch, would be a cause of death,
A force sufficient to dissolve in air
Textures of mortal substance. But here's the fact—
The elements are held, are bound together
In different degrees, but the basic stuff
Is indestructible, so things remain
Intact, unharmed, until a force is found
Proportionate to their texture, to effect
Reversion to their primal elements,
But never to complete annihilation.

Finally, when the fathering air has poured
His rainfall into mother earth, the drops
Seem to have gone, but look!—bright harvests rise,
Boughs on the trees bring greenery and growth
And are weighed down by fruit, by which, in turn,
Our race is fed, and so are animals,
And we see happy cities, flowering
With children, and we hear the music rise
As new birds sing all through the leafy woods.
Fat cows lie down to rest their weary sides
In welcome pastures, and the milk drops white
Out of distended udders; and the calves
Romp over the tender grass, or wobble, drunk
On that pure vintage, more than strong enough
For any such experience as theirs.
To sum it up: no visible object dies;
Nature from one thing brings another forth,
And out of death new life is born.

                            Now then—
I have shown that things can never be created
From nothing, and that no created thing
Can ever be called back to nothingness.
You may, perhaps, begin to doubt my lessons
Since atoms are too small to see, but listen,—
You must admit that there are other bodies
Existing but invisible.

                        The wind
Beats ocean with its violence, overwhelms
Great ships, sends the clouds flying, or at times
Sweeps over land with a tornado's fury,
Strewing the plains with trees, and beating mountains
With forest-shattering blasts; its roaring howls
Aloud and wild, and even its mutter threatens.
Surely, most surely, the winds are unseen bodies,
Sweepers of earth and sea and sky, and whirlers
Of sudden hurricane. They flow, they flood,
They breed destruction just the way a river
Of gentle nature swells to a great deluge
By the increase of rainfall from the mountains,
Commingling in ruin broken brush and trees.
Strong bridges cannot hold the sudden fury
Of water coming on; the river, darkened
By the great rain, dashes against the piles
With mighty force, and with a mighty sound
Roars on, destroying; under its current it rolls
Tremendous rocks; it sweeps away whatever
Resists its surge. So the wind's blast must also
Be a strong river, a fall of devastation
Wherever it goes, shoving some things before it,
Attacking over and over, in eddy and whirl,
Having its way, seizing and carrying things.
I tell you again and again, the winds are bodies
Invisible, they are rivals of great rivers
In what they do and are, though rivers, of course,
Are something we can see.

And what of odors?
We sense them, but we never see them coming
Toward our nostrils; we do not look at heat,
Apprehend cold with our eyes, we are not accustomed
To witness voices. Yet all these things, by nature,
Must be material, since they strike our senses.
Nothing can touch or be touched, excepting matter.

Then, too—if you spread your clothes along a shore
Where waves are breaking, they'll get wet, but they'll dry
If you hang them in the sun. Have we ever watched
The moisture settle in, or the way it flees
In warmth? It must disperse, must be fragmented
In particles too fine for our eyes to see.

Also, as years go through their revolutions
A ring wears thin under the finger's touch,
The drip of water hollows the stone, the plough
With its curving iron slowly wastes away
In the field it works; the footsteps of the people
We see wear out the paving-stones of rock
In the city streets, and at the city gates
Bronze statues show their right hands, thinner and thinner
From the touch of passers-by, through years of greeting.
We see these things worn down, diminished, only
After long lapse of time; nature denies us
The sight we need for any given moment.

And finally: what nature adds to things,
Little by little, forcing them to growth,
No marshalled tenseness of our gaze can see.
When things corrode with leanness and old age,
When tiny salt eats into great sea cliffs,
You cannot see the process of the loss
At any given moment. Nature's work
Is done by means of particles unseen.

But not all bodily matter is tight-packed
By nature's law, for there's a void in things.

This knowledge will be useful to you often,
Will keep you from the path of doubt, from asking
Too many questions on the sum of things,
From losing confidence in what I tell you.
By *void* I mean vacant and empty space,
Something you cannot touch. Were this not so,
Things could not move. The property of matter,
Its most outstanding trait, is to stand firm,
Its office to oppose; and everything
Would always be immovable, since matter
Never gives way. But with our eyes we see
Many things moving, in their wondrous ways,
Their marvelous means, through sea and land and sky.
Were there no void, they would not only lack
This restlessness of motion altogether,
But more than that—they never could have been
Quickened to life from that tight-packed quiescence.

Besides, however solid things appear,
Let me show you proof that even these are porous:
In a cave of rocks the seep of moisture trickles
And the whole place weeps its fat blobs of tears.
Food is dispersed all through a creature's body;
Young trees grow tall and yield their fruit in season,
Drawing their sustenance from the lowest roots
Through trunks and branches; voices penetrate
Walls and closed doors; the seep of stiffening cold
Permeates bone. Phenomena like these
Would be impossible but for empty spaces
Where particles can pass. And finally,
Why do we see that some things outweigh others
Which are every bit as large? If a ball of wool
Has the same substance as a ball of lead,
(Assuming the dimensions are the same)
They both should weigh as much, since matter tends
To exercise a constant downward pressure.
But void lacks weight. So, when two objects bulk
The same, but one is obviously lighter,

It clearly states its greater share of void,
And, on the other hand, the heavier thing
Proclaims it has less void and greater substance.
Certainly, therefore, what we're looking for
By logical deduction, does exist,
Is mixed with solid, and we call it *void*.

I must anticipate a little here
Lest you succumb to some folks' foolishness.
They claim that water opens a clear path
To the nosing fish, because the latter leave
Spaces behind them into which the waves
Can flow together again, and others things,
Likewise, can move, in reciprocity
Exchanging places, though every place is taken.
What nonsense! What direction can the fish
Find for their progress, unless the water yields,
And to what place will the water be enabled
To find its way again, if fish can't move?
All bodies, then, must lack the power of movement,
Or you must grant that there's a void in things
From which each one derives its motive impulse.
Finally, if you see two good-sized bodies
Bounce off each other quickly, after contact,
Then surely air must occupy the space
Which they have left, and though it rushes in
With utmost speed, it cannot all at once
Fill the whole area, but "First things first!",
"One at a time!", till all the space is filled.
Someone may think that bodies leap apart
Because the air that lies between them thickens.
That's a mistake: for that there'd have to be
A void, not there before, and a filled-up space
That formerly was void. In no such way
Can atmosphere condense; it must have void.

For all your "Yes, but—" dragging of the heels,
You'll have to come at last to this admission,—

Void does exist. I could mention many things,
Pile up a heap of argument-building proof,
But why? You have some sense, and these few hints
Ought to suffice. You can find out for yourself.
As mountain-ranging hounds smell out a lair,
An animal's covert, hidden under brush,
Once they are certain of its track, so you,
All by yourself, in matters such as these,
Can see one thing from another, find your way
To the dark burrows and bring truth to light.
But if you lag or shrink, even a little,
Memmius, this I promise you for sure:
My honeyed tongue from my rich heart will pour
Such inexhaustible potions from its sources
That slow old age, I fear, will penetrate
Our limbs, loosen our life-bonds, and the deluge
Of my argument in verse still flood your ears
Over one item only.

             Now to repeat:
The nature of everything is dual—matter
And void; or particles and space, wherein
The former rest or move. We have our senses
To tell us matter exists. Denying this,
We cannot, searching after hidden things,
Find any base of reason whatsoever.
Next, if there is no place, or space, our so-called void,
Bodies could nowhere be, and nowhere move.
I proved this not so long ago, remember.
Also, there's nothing else which you can call
Distinct alike from matter and from void,
Some kind of, maybe, third alternative.
No. What exists is something in itself,
Susceptible to touch, however frail,
However tiny, and capable of growth,
Of increase after its fashion. But a something
Touch cannot reach, a thing that cannot keep
Another thing from simply passing through it,

This kind of thing must be our so-called void.
Besides, if something has its own existence,
It will either act itself, or, being passive,
Will suffer other things to act upon it,
Or yield a space where things can be, or happen,
But nothing without substance has the power
To act, or to be acted on, and nothing
Can proffer space except the void and empty.
Therefore, except for void and substance, nothing,
No third alternative, no other nature
Can possibly exist in the sum of things,
Perceptible to any of our senses
Or apprehended by the reasoning mind.

Whatever exists you will always find connected
To these two things, or as by-products of them;
Connected meaning that the quality
Can never be subtracted from its object
No more than weight from stone, or heat from fire,
Wetness from water. On the other hand,
Slavery, riches, freedom, poverty,
War, peace, and so on, transitory things
Whose comings and goings do not alter substance—
These, and quite properly, we call *by-products.*
Time also has no separate existence,
But present, past, and future reach our senses
From what occurs, by-products of by-products.
We must admit that no man's sense of time
Exists apart from things at rest or moving,
So when people talk about the rape of Helen,
Of Troy subdued in war, beware, don't let them
Convince us that such things were entities,
Since ages past recall have taken away
The human generations, whose by-products
The wars and Helen were. The term applies
Alike to human beings and to places,
And, finally,—if things had had no substance
Nor space where acts occur, the passionate fire

Burning in Paris' heart would not have kindled
The savage war's bright battles; the Greek horse
Would never have loosed the night-born soldiery
To set the town on fire. So you can see
That actions never exist all by themselves
As matter does, or void, but rather are
By-products, both of matter and of space.

Bodies are partly basic elements
Of things, and partly compounds of the same.
The basic elements no force can shatter
Since, being solid, they resist destruction.
Yet it seems difficult to believe that objects
Are ever found to be completely solid.
A thunderbolt goes through the walls of houses,
As noise and voices do, and iron whitens
In fire, and steam at boiling point splits rocks,
Gold's hardnesses are pliant under heat,
The ice of bronze melts in the flame, and silver
Succumbs to warmth or chill, as our senses tell us
With the cup in our hands, and water, hot or cold,
Poured into the wine. No, there is nothing solid
In things, or so it seems; reason, however,
And science are compelling forces—therefore
Stay with me; it will not take many verses
For me to explain that there are things with bodies
Solid and everlasting; these we call
Seeds of things, firstlings, atoms, and in them lies
The sum of all created things.

                              To start with,
Since it has been established that the nature
Of things is different, dual, one being substance,
The other void, it follows that each one
Must, in its essence, be itself completely.
Where space exists, or what we call the void,
Matter cannot be found; what substance holds
Void cannot occupy. So atoms are

Solid and therefore voidless. Furthermore,
If there is void in things, there has to be
Solid material surrounding this.
Nothing, by logic, can be proved to hold
A void within its mass, unless you grant
It must itself be solid. There can be
Nothing except an organized composure
Of matter, which can hold a void within it.
And matter, therefore, being of solid substance,
Can last forever, while all else is shattered.
Then, were there nothing which we label *void*,
All would be solid substance; and again,
Were there no substance to fill up the spaces,
All would be void and emptiness. These, then,
Must alternate, substance and void, since neither
Exists to the exclusion of the other.
So there is substance, which marks off the limits
Between the full and the empty, and this substance
Cannot be broken if blows are struck against it
From anywhere outside it, not exploded
By dissolution from within, nor weakened
In any other way, as I have shown you.
It must be obvious that, lacking void,
Nothing can possibly be crushed or broken
Or split in two by cutting, or allow
Invasion by water, cold, or fire, those forces
Of dissolution. The more an object holds
Void space within it, the more easily
It weakens under stress and strain; and therefore,
As I have pointed out, when stuff is solid,
Without that void, it must be everlasting.
Were this not true of matter, long ago
Everything would have crumbled into nothing
And things we see today have been restored
From nothing; but remember, I have proved
Nothing can be created out of nothing.
Also, that nothing can be brought to nothing.
So basic elements must be immortal,

Impossible to dissolve in some last moment
Else there would be no matter for renewal.
They must be, then, completely singly solid,
For otherwise they could not through the ages
Be kept intact for restoration's work

Moreover, if nature had not set a limit
To fragmentation, by this time all matter
Would have been so reduced by time's attrition
That not one thing could move from a beginning
To full, completed growth. We see that objects
Can be broken up more quickly than put together,
So the long day, the everlasting process
Of all past time, disturbing and dissolving,
Could not, by now, nor even in the future,
Have ever repaired its damage. But we see
Each thing restored, each with its time and season
For flowering, so, we conclude, there must be
A sure and certain limit to its breaking.

Another thing: material particles
Are solid, absolutely, yet we can
Account for softnesses in things like air,
Water, and earth, and fire; they are what they are
Since void is part of them. On the other hand,
If basic stuff were soft, no explanation
Accounts for hard material like flint
Or iron, since all nature, so, would lack
A solid point to start with. Therefore, things
Are strong by single solid unity,
But all things can, by denser combination,
Be packed more tightly, and display more strength.
Moreover, if no end is ever set
To break-up, still things must and do remain
After the long eternity of time,
Assailed by never a danger. How? It seems
Ridiculous to argue that they could
Resist forever, if their nature were

Acknowledged to be fragile. Finally,
Since it is now agreed that creatures have
A limit to their times of growth and life,
Their laws of nature telling what they can
And cannot do, immutable laws, so fixed
That all the varicolored birds have markings
Like others of their kind; therefore, they must have
Identical basic bodies. Otherwise,
If first-beginnings could be changed at whim,
There would be no assurance what can be
And what cannot, limits and boundaries,
Systems determined and immutable,
Nor could the generations reproduce
Parental nature, habits, diets, movements.

Now, every single substance has some point
Which seems to us the smallest, so there must
By the same logic be some smallest point
In particles our senses cannot see.
This has no parts, it cannot be divided,
It is an ultimate, has no existence
Entirely of its own, and never will have,
Being in its essential nature part
Of something else primordial and basic
Whence, more and more, other such parts fill out
The basic structure by their thickened mass.
These particles, incapable themselves
Of separate status, are held together,
Are indissoluble by any force.
So, any atom has a singleness
Solid, coherent, not compound, but strong
In its eternal singleness and nature
Which keeps it as a seed of things, allows
No diminution nor subtraction from it.

Something must be the smallest that there is.
Otherwise, every possible tiny object
Will be composed of infinite particles,

A half can always be in halves divided,
No limit to all this. So how would they differ,
The universe from the littlest thing? They wouldn't,
For if the total is divisible
Ad infinitum, then the smallest objects
Would likewise be so. But since reason tells us
This makes no sense, we therefore must acknowledge
That there are things which have no parts at all,
The smallest natural objects. This being so,
It follows that they are solid and eternal.
Lastly, if the creative force of nature
Had always caused all objects to be broken
Into the smallest particles, nature would not
Have power to restore them, since they'd lack
Such parts as have the power of generation,
Connections, weight and impact, clash and motion,
Through which all things establish their behavior.

Now, those who think the essence of all things
Is fire, and fire alone, are worse than foolish,
For example, Heraclitus, that great captain
Whose fame is bright because of his dark speech,
More so, of course, among the empty-headed
Than earnest Greek researchers after truth.
Fools have more love and admiration, always
For things their blindness sees in hidden meanings;
They base their truths on what can sometimes tickle
Their ears, or what is soaked in sweetish sound.

I ask you: why can objects vary so
If they are all created out of fire,
Fire pure and simple? And you cannot argue
That fire, being hot, is ever thickened or thinned
If the parts, by nature, are the same as the whole.
Heat should increase if the parts are brought together,
Diminish with separation; nothing else
Is possible to suppose under such conditions,
Nor could such great variety of things

Be in proportion as fire is thick or thin.
Another thing: if your Stoics grant that void
Is mixed with things, then fire of course can thicken
Or thin; the trouble with holding to this notion
Is that they see too many things in conflict,
Shun recognition of a void in things,
Fear the steep road, and therefore lose the true one.
Nor do they see, that if a void is lacking
In things, then all must be condensed together,
All form one mass, unable to throw out
Anything from itself in quick discharge,
As a hot fire throws out both light and steam.
But if they think that in some other way
Fires can be doused, change character and being,
They are also bound to argue that this process
Keeps happening all the time, and fire will vanish
Someday completely, and all created things
Come back to birth from nothing. But a substance
So changed that it forsakes its former nature
Becomes the death of what it was before.
They will have to leave these substances a something
Residual, intact, or else acknowledge
That all things utterly return to nothing
And out of nothing comes rebirth. What nonsense!
In fact, however, nothing is more certain
Than that some bodies do preserve their nature
In the same way forever, and their goings,
Their comings, and their changed arrangements fashion
Whatever change there is. We may be sure
These elements are not composed of fire.
It would make no sense if some things were subtracted
And others added, or positions changed,
If every thing were of a fiery nature,
For everything thus made would still be fiery.
The truth, I think, is this: there are certain bodies
Whose meeting, motion, order, shape, position
Do produce fire; when this relation changes
Their nature changes. They are not like fire

Nor any other object with the power
To send forth particles, and by their impact
Affect our sense of touch.

                          To go beyond this,
To say all things are fire, that there's nothing, really,
In all the world but fire—(as this same fellow
Insists)—why, this is absolutely mad.
He draws his argument against the senses
From these same senses, shatters the foundations
From which beliefs arise, the very source
Whence he himself perceives this thing called fire.
The senses, he concedes, do recognize
Fire, no mistake about it, but they fail
In their regard (says he) of other things
Never a bit less bright and clear. This seems
Not only silly, but mad. Where shall we turn?
What can there be more certain than our senses
To mark true things and false? So why remove
All things but fire, and say that fire alone
Exists? Why not argue the other way,
Say fire does not exist, but everything else does?
Such logic would be no more idiotic.

Others have erred: the ones who think that air
Is the prime element of all creation,
Or those who think that water is, or earth,
Source of creation and change. Mistaken also
Are those who say two elements must pair,
The air and fire, water and earth; or double
The doubling, and insist that all things come
Out of four elements, earth, air, fire, water.
One of their greatest is Empedocles,
A man from Agrigentum; he was born
On that three-cornered island, where the surge
Of the grey-green Ionian sprays and spatters
Along a jagged coast-line, and the strait
Races with rushing water that divides

Italy from the island. Vast Charybdis
Roars here below Mt. Etna's rumble and threat
Of flame belched up to sky, and flash and thunder.
Oh, a great wonder, in more ways than one,
And men should come to see it, as they do,
A land rich in good things, and fortified
By a great store of heroes, none renowned
More than Empedocles, and nothing there,
More holy, more remarkable, more dear.
His poems are godlike, and they cry aloud,
Announce such glorious findings that he seems
Scarcely a mortal being.

                       But he was wrong,
He and his followers (much lesser men).
In spite of all their findings, spoken well,
With holier wisdom and sense than oracles
From Pythian tripod and Apollo's laurel,
Down they came crashing, for their false ideas
Of origin brought them low; great men they were,
And greatly fallen. They insist that motion
Is an inherent attribute of things,
But that void is lacking; things are soft, or open
In texture, they allow, for example, air,
Mist, fire, and earth, its creatures and its harvests,
But they deny any void within these bodies.
Their next mistake ensues because they set
No limit to the process of division,
No end to break-up; they deny to fractions
An ultimately least. You know our senses
Can recognize what seems to be the height
Of littleness in anything; from this
It ought to follow that beyond the range
Of sense there lies an ultimate end, a point
Which actually is the smallest. Furthermore
They say the first beginnings of things are soft,
Whereas soft things, we know, are born, and die,
So that, were these men right, the sum of things

Would long ago have gone to nothingness,
And out of nothingness come back to life,
Flourishing, vigorous. How wrong this is
You have been taught already. Furthermore,
These elements of theirs are enemies,
In many ways they are hostile to each other
So that their clash should either be their death,
Or their collision diffuse them, as a storm
Makes winds, rain, lightning fly in all directions.

If, out of four things, all things are created,
If, into four things, all things are resolved,
How can these four be called the source? Why not
The other way around? They take their turn
In being born, it seems, they change complexion,
Change their whole nature all the time. Now, really,
Can you believe that fire, earth, air, and water
So fuse that nothing changes in their fusion?
If so, how could they make you some new creature,
Animate, or inanimate like a tree?
Each element in this conglomerate pile-up
Will show its nature, air be seen to mingle
With earth, and fire be visible with water.
But first-beginnings, in producing things,
Should keep their own peculiar nature hidden,
Secret, out of sight, lest some appearance
Of their own quality war and fight against
New substance being born in its own image.

The Stoics are even worse. They start with heaven
And heaven's fires, and say that fire first changes
Into the winds of air; this causes water,
And water produces earth, then back again,
Air into fire, the same way up and down.
But basic elements should not act like this,
Something must stand immovable, it must,
Lest all things be reduced to absolute nothing.
If anything is changed, leaving its limits,

That is the death of what it was before.
So, since the things we mentioned earlier come
Into a change, they must, beyond a doubt,
Consist of other things which never change,
Else all would be reduced to absolute nothing.
It would be better, would it not, to reason
Some bodies are endowed with such a nature
They can make fire, or, with some giving and taking,
—Add this, subtract a little of that—can form
The winds of air, and all the variations?

"But," you are saying, "it's a patent fact
That into the winds of the air, out of the earth,
All things are given increase and nourishment,
And unless weather is kindly with its rainfall
At the right time, so that the trees will sway
Backward and forward under the waste of cloud,
And unless the sun, at the right time, fondly gives them
His warmth again, nothing could grow, no grain,
No trees, no animals." Perfectly true,
And were we men not helped by food and water,
The moist and the dry, our bodies soon would perish,
All life depart from all our bones and sinews.
Of course we are helped, of course, of course, we are nourished
By certain definite things; all creatures are,
In different ways, of course. The reason is
That many things have elements in common,
But differently combined; and therefore nurture
Must also differ. It is most important
Both with what other elements they are joined,
In what positions they are held together,
And their reciprocal movement. The same atoms
Constitute ocean, sky, lands, rivers, sun,
Crops, bushes, animals; these atoms mingle
And move in different ways and combinations.
Look—in my lines here you can see the letters
Common to many of the words, but you know
Perfectly well that resonance and meaning,

Sense, sound, are changed by changing the arrangement.
How much more true of atoms than of letters!

Now for a look at Anaxagoras,
Whose theory, to coin a word, we'll call
Likepartedness, an awkward-sounding term,
But clear enough in illustration: bones
Are made of very tiny little bonelets,
And flesh of infinitesimal bits of flesh,
And blood of many many wee drops of blood,
Gold from gold grains, and earth from earthen motes,
Fire out of fire, and moisture out of moisture,
Well, everything from its *likepartedness*.
What he does not allow is void in things;
He puts no limit to their subdivision.
In both these points he seems to me in error
As well as in his general argument.
His elements, atoms, first-beginnings, are
By far too frail; you can't apply such terms
To things which pass away like their creations,
Are equally destructible. Which of them
Endures between the upper and lower millstones,
Lives in the jaws of death? Fire? Water? Earth?
Blood? Bone? Not one, not one whose particles
Are of the same doomed stuff that we can see
Annihilated while we watch. But matter,
As I have proved before, can never be
Reduced to nothing, so, nor things created
From nothing.

                    Furthermore, since food
Nourishes bodies, makes them grow, it follows
That veins and blood and bones and nerves and sinews
Are made by things unlike themselves. Perhaps
They'll try to get around this fact by saying
That food is made of elements in mixture,
Contains small particles of blood, bone, sinew—
If so, then food, both moist and dry, is composed

Of things unlike itself, bone, lymph, and nerves.
Besides, whatever bodies grow from earth,
If they are in the earth, let's say, to start with,
Why, then, earth must consist of things unearthly
Which rise from earth. Or change the metaphor:
If flame lies hidden in wood, with smoke and ashes,
Then wood consists of things un-wooden, surely,
Exactly as with earth.

There's a way out,
And Anaxagoras is quick to take it,
Thinking all things lie hidden in all things,
But only one appears, that being the one
Whose particles are most numerous, or perhaps
The most conspicuous, most near the surface.
This does not make much sense; it ought to follow
That corn when ground between the turning millstones
Should give some sign of blood, or at least something
Whereby our bodies are nourished. Grind stone on stone,
Blood ought to trickle out. In the same way
Crushed grass should give sweet drops of milk, in flavor
Like that from woolly sheep, and crumbled clods
Ought to show grass or twigs in miniature,
And smoke and ash emerge from broken faggots.
The simple facts say *"No!"* to all such error.
This cannot be the way it is, but still
There must be basic elements in common
In many things, unseen, but surely there.
"But," you object, "often in mighty mountains
High boughs of neighboring trees by the strong winds
Are caused to rub their surfaces together
Till they break out in flame." Yes, certainly;
But fire's not actually hidden in the wood,
Though there are fire-producing particles
Whose friction lights whole forests. If the flame
Were actually there, in its pure state, but hidden,
Those fires could not for long be kept a secret,
They would break out, they would put an end to forests,

Set every bush ablaze. So now you see
What I have said before, it is most important
Both with what other elements they are joined,
In what position they are held together
And their reciprocal movement. Just as in spelling
A little change makes all the difference:
Subtract an -E, and *fire* is changed to *fir*.
To end this argument—if you suppose
Whatever you see contains, in microcosm,
Likepartedness of little parts, if men
Are made up of homunculi, farewell
To any sensible theory of atoms.
The little men inside you will be roaring
With mirth till tears run down their cheeks.

                         Come, come,
Listen to what is left, and hear more clearly:
I know how dark and difficult things are,
But the high hope of praise has moved my heart
As if by the wave of a wand, and deep within
Filled me with sweet devotion to the Muses.
Almost by instinct now, with mind alert,
I range those pathless groves, where no one ever
Has gone before me, and I come to fountains
Completely undefiled, I drink their waters,
Delight myself by gathering new flowers,
Fashioning out of them a kind of garland
No Muse, before this time, has ever given
To crown a human being. I teach great things,
I try to loose men's spirit from the ties,
Tight-knotted, which religion binds around them.
The Muses' grace is on me, as I write
Clear verse about dark matters. This is not
A senseless affectation; there's reason to it.
Just as when doctors try to give to children
A bitter medicine, they rim the cup
With honey's sweetness, honey's golden flavor,
To fool the silly little things, as far

As the lips at least, so that they'll take the bitter
Dosage, and swallow it down, fooled, but not swindled,
But brought to health again through double-dealing,
So now do I, because this doctrine seems
Too grim for those who never yet have tried it,
So grim that people shrink from it, I've meant
To explain the system in a sweeter music,
To rim the lesson, as it were, with honey,
Hoping, this way, to hold your mind with verses
While you are learning all that form, that pattern
Of the way things are.

                 I have already taught you
That matter's basic elements are solid,
Completely so, and that they fly through time
Invincible, indestructible for ever.
Now let's work out whether there's any limit
To their sum total; study, likewise, void,
Space, emptiness, area where all things move.
Does this have finite limits or does it reach
Unmeasurable in deep wide boundlessness?
The universe is limitless, unbounded
In any of its areas; otherwise
It would have to have an end somewhere, but no—
Nothing, it seems, can possibly have an end
Without there being something out beyond it,
Beyond perception's range. We must admit
There can be nothing beyond the sum of things,
Therefore that sum is infinite, limitless.
It makes no difference where you stand, your center
Permits of no circumference around it.
Assume, though, for a moment, that all space
Is definitely limited, what happens
If somebody runs to its furthest rim, and rifles
A javelin outward? Will it keep on going,
Full force, or do you think something can stop it?
Here's a dilemma that you can't escape!
You have to grant an infinite universe

For either there's matter there, to stop our spear,
Or space through which it keeps on flying. Right?
So it wasn't flung from any boundary line.
I will keep after you with this argument, ask you,
No matter where you set the outermost limit,
What happens to the javelin after that?
The answer is that a final boundary line
Is nowhere in existence, there will always
Be plenty of room beyond for the spear's flight.
Before our eyes, thing seems to limit thing,
Air bounds the hills, and forests border air,
Earth sea, sea earth, but add them up, and nothing
Limits the sum.

                    Besides, if all the space
Of all the universe were fixed, enclosed
By definite bounds, by this time all the mass,
The weight, of matter would have run together
From all sides to the bottom, tending downward
From the sheer force of weight, so there could be
No room for action under heaven's roof,
No heaven, for that matter, and no sun,
Since all material would be heaped so high
From its long subsidence through endless time.
But as it is, no rest is ever given
To the atoms' rainfall; there's no pit, far down,
To be their pool, their ultimate resting-place.
All things keep on, in everlasting motion,
Out of the infinite come the particles
Speeding above, below, in endless dance.
By nature space is deep and space is boundless,
So that bright shafts of lightning could not cross it,
Given eternal time, nor could they lessen
The area before their onward course.
There is too much space, all here and there, around them,
No limit to that infinite domain.

And nature will not have it that the sum
Of things set any limits for themselves,

Forcing matter to be limited
By void, and void be limited by matter.
This alternation, this recurrence, makes
The total limitless. One or the other,
Were it not for this, would singly spread itself
Out of all moderation. Matter and space,
I say again, are equally infinite,
Else neither sea nor land nor shining sky,
Neither human beings nor high gods incarnate
Could stay beyond the passing of a moment,
For matter, driven from its normal fusion,
Loosed beyond all abundance, would come sweeping
Through the great emptiness, or, far more likely,
Would never have created anything,
Never have been compacted from disorder.
Surely the atoms never began by forming
A conscious pact, a treaty with each other,
Where they should stay apart, where come together.
More likely, being so many, in many ways
Harassed and driven through the universe
From an infinity of time, by trying
All kinds of motion, every combination,
They came at last into such disposition
As now establishes the sum of things.
And this arrangement, kept through cosmic cycles,
Each one ten thousand years, would make the rivers
Flood, glut with waves insatiable ocean deeps,
Earth, fondled by sun's warmness, bring to birth
New generations, and the wheeling fires
Of heaven endure. Now this could not be done
If there were not an infinite supply
Of matter, whence lost things could be restored,
Each in its proper season. Any beast
Deprived of food will die; so all things must
Succumb to dissolution, once the source
Dries up replenishment. Blows from without
Cannot, by pressure, save the sum of things.
They'll batter away, they'll keep on battering,
Keep parts intact till new replacements come,

But, even so, at times they must rebound,
Yield time and space for atoms to fly free
Out of their old composure. Over and over,
Even for blows like these to keep on coming,
We need an infinite quantity of matter.

One thing they'll tell you, Memmius; don't believe it,
And that's the argument that all things tend
Toward a center; hence the world stands firm
Without external pressure; high things or low
Can't be turned loose, go flying every which way,
Since matter is compelled to seek the center—
(Well, maybe so, at least if you believe
That anything can stand on top of itself)—
Things weighty, below earth, will rise again
And rest on earth, but upside down, like trees
We see reflected in a glassy river.
Likewise, of course, earth's animals all walk
Head down—can't fall into the sky below
Any more than we can rise to tracts of heaven.
When they see sun, we see the stars of night.
Their nights, our days, go by in alternation.
How stupid! How ridiculous! How can
There be a center in the infinite?
And even if there were, how could things stay there?
If space and void exist, they must yield passage
Wherever they are, through center or non-center,
To moving substance, nowhere, never, a place
Where bodies come to weightlessness and stop
In everlasting standstill. By its nature
Void cannot offer rest, but only passage.
Impossible, therefore, that things combine
In a compulsive frenzy toward a center.

Besides, they do not claim that all things press
Centerward so, but only earth and water,
Things, so to speak, of earthy frame—our bodies—
Or watery—like sea's weight, or mountain cascades.

It differs with thin air and with hot fire:
They claim that these are driven *from* the center,
And therefore heaven blinks with constellations,
And fire goes grazing over the blue sky-pastures,
Because heat flees the center, gathers there.
Otherwise tops of trees could hardly live,
Being so far from earth, unless some food
Could come to them a little at a time
Supplied from earth below.*
This must be wrong. The ramparts of the world
Would otherwise vanish, suddenly dissolved,
As flames disperse in utter emptiness,
And all things in like manner come to ruin,
The thundering areas of sky collapse,
Earth crumble underfoot, and in the wrack
Of sky and all things, loosened and confounded,
All perish, all, and in one flick of time
Nothing be left but desert, chaos, darkness.
For in whatever part you predicate
An absence of atomic stuff, be sure
That part will be the gate of death, that way
The portal for destruction, mass and matter
Rushing headlong to doom.

                    If you know this,
It only takes a very little trouble
To learn the rest: the lessons, one by one,
Brighten each other, no dark night will keep you,
Pathless, astray, from ultimate vision and light,
All things illumined in each other's radiance.

* Some lines here have been dropped from the archetypal ms. Their sense
must have been to ridicule the theory with further illustration.

Book II

How sweet it is, when whirlwinds roil great ocean,
To watch, from land, the danger of another,
Not that to see some other person suffer
Brings great enjoyment, but the sweetness lies
In watching evils you yourself are free from.
How sweet, again, to see the clash of battle
Across the plains, yourself immune to danger.
But nothing is more sweet than full possession
Of those calm heights, well built, well fortified
By wise men's teaching, to look down from here
At others wandering below, men lost,
Confused, in hectic search for the right road,
The strife of wits, the wars for precedence,
The everlasting struggle, night and day,
To win towards heights of wealth and power. O wretched,
O wretched minds of men! O hearts in darkness!
Under what shadows and among what dangers
Your lives are spent, such as they are. But look—
Your nature snarls, yaps, barks for nothing, really,
Except that pain be absent from the body
And mind enjoy delight, with fear dispelled,
Anxiety gone. We do not need so much
For bodily comfort, only loss of pain.
I grant you, luxuries are very pleasant,
But nature does not really care if houses
Lack golden statues in the halls, young men
Holding out fiery torches in their hands
To light the all-night revels. Let the house
Gleam silver and gold, the music waken echoes
In gilded panel and crossbeam—never mind.

Much poorer men are every bit as happy,
Are quite well-off, stretched out in groups together
On the soft grass beside a running brook,
Under a tall tree's shade, in lovely weather,
Where flowers star green meadows. Fever's heat
Departs no sooner if your bodies toss
On crimson sheets, or under figured covers,
Than if you have to lie on a poor blanket.
So, since our bodies find in wealth no profit,
And none in rank or power, it must be mind
Is no more profited. You may see your hosts
Make mimic wars, surging across the drill-ground,
Flanked by their cavalry and well-supported
By strong reserves, high in morale. You may
Behold your fleet churn wide across great seas—
And does all this frighten religious terror
In panic from your heart? does the great fear
Of death depart, and leave you comforted?
What vanity, what nonsense! If men's fears,
Anxieties, pursuing horrors, move,
Indifferent to any clash of arms,
Untroubled among lords and monarchs, bow
Before no gleam of gold, no crimson robe,
Why do you hesitate, why doubt that reason
Alone has absolute power? Our life is spent
In shadows, and it suffers in the dark.
As children tremble and fear everything
In their dark shadows, we, in the full light,
Fear things that really are not one bit more awful
Than what poor babies shudder at in darkness,
The horrors they imagine to be coming.
Our terrors and our darknesses of mind
Must be dispelled, then, not by sunshine's rays,
Not by those shining arrows of the light,
But by insight into nature, and a scheme
Of systematic contemplation. Come,
Let me explain what kind of movement causes
The life-producing elements to beget

All kinds of things, and, when they are begotten,
To loosen them from life, what force impels them
To act this way, to give them power to move
Through the great void: remember, pay attention!
Matter surely does not cohere, tight-packed,
Since we can see that everything is lessened,
Can see all things flowing away with time,
Whose slow attrition takes them from our sight,
While still the sum of things remains intact.
Whatever is subtracted from one thing
Is added to another. In their course
The seeds of things cause fading, or cause bloom,
And never linger; so the sum of things
Is constantly renewed, all creatures live
In symbiosis, or, in homelier terms,
On a see-saw up and down, or an infinite relay,
Each generation, like a runner, handing
The torch on to another.

                              If you think
Atoms can stop their course, refrain from movement,
And by cessation cause new kinds of motion,
You are far astray indeed. Since there is void
Through which they move, all fundamental motes
Must be impelled, either by their own weight
Or by some force outside them. When they strike
Each other, they bounce off; no wonder, either,
Since they are absolute solid, all compact,
With nothing back of them to block their path.
To help you see more clearly that all atoms
Are always moving, just remember this:
There is no bottom to the universe,
No place for basic particles to rest,
Since space is infinite, unlimited,
Reaching beyond all bounds, in all directions,
As time and time again I have shown you proof.
Therefore, of course, no atom ever rests
Coming through void, but always drives, is driven

In various ways, and their collisions cause,
As the case may be, greater or less rebound.
When they are held in thickest combination,
At closer intervals, with the space between
More hindered by their interlock of figure,
These give us rock, or adamant, or iron,
Things of that nature. (Not very many kinds
Go wandering little and lonely through the void.)
There are some whose alternate meetings, partings, are
At greater intervals; from these we are given
Thin air, the shining sunlight. Many more
Have been kept out of any combination,
Nowhere conjoin. Before our eyes we have
An illustration. If you look sometimes,
You see the motes all dancing, as the sun
Streams through the shutters into a dark room.
Look!—there they go, like armies in maneuver
Whose little squadrons charge, retreat, join, part,
From this you can deduce that on a scale
Oh, infinitely smaller, beyond your sight,
Similar turbulence whirls. A little thing
Can often show us what a great one's like,
And that's not all the story, either. Watch!—
Those motes in the sunlight, by their restlessness,
Tell you there's motion, hidden and unseen,
In what seems solid matter. As they bounce,
Change course, come back, here, there, and every which way,
You may be sure this restlessness is given
By their essential core, atomic essence,
From just these first-beginnings. They are moved
By their own inner impulse first, and then
Such groups as form with just a few together,
Only a little bigger than their units,
Are moved by unseen blows from these: in turn
They shove along the somewhat larger masses.
So, motion comes from first-beginnings, grows
By slow degrees till we can see the process,
Just as we see the dancing motes in the sunlight,

But cannot see what urge compels the dancing.

Now then—what kind of speed does matter have?
The answer, Memmius, won't take very long.
When dawn bathes earth with morning light, and birds,
All kinds of them, flying through pathless woods,
Fill all the delicate air with liquid song,
How suddenly at such a time the sun
Clothes everything with light! This we can see,
And so can all men, plain before their eyes.
But the sun's warmth and that calm light come on
Not through an empty void; their course is set
More slowly, as if they parted waves of air
The way a swimmer does. Not one by one
Do the tiny particles of heat proceed,
But rather *en masse*, get in each other's way,
At times, and are also blocked by outside force.
All this combines to make them go more slowly.
It does not work this way with single atoms
Which go along through empty void, unchecked
By opposition. They have their parts, of course,
But they are single units; they drive on,
Resistless, toward their first direction's impulse,
And they must be of marvelous speed, beyond
The speed of light, surpassing far the sweep
Of lightning in split seconds through the sky—
Impossible to follow every atom,
To see complete their order, action, system.

Some people do not know how matter works.
They think that nature needs the will of the gods
To fit the seasons of the year so nicely
To human needs, to bring to birth the crops
And other blessings, which our guide to life,
The radiance of pleasure, makes us crave
Through Venus' agency. To be sure, we breed
To keep the race alive, but to think that gods
Have organized all things for the sake of men

Is nothing but a lot of foolishness.
I might not know a thing about the atoms,
But this much I can say, from what I see
Of heaven's ways and many other features:
The nature of the world just could not be
A product of the gods' devising; no,
There are too many things the matter with it.
I'll give you further details, Memmius, later.
Now to get on with further explanation
Concerning motion.

             The first point to make
Is, no internal force can make things rise
Or force them upward. Don't be fooled by sparks:
I know they rise, increase, grow upward; crops
Act the same way, and trees, although their weight
Exerts a downward pull. We must not think,
When fires go leaping toward the roofs of houses,
And the swift flames lick out at beams and timbers,
That they do this of their own will entirely,
Without the urge of pressure from below.
Blood acts the same way, spurting from our bodies,
Arterial jets, a scarlet-colored fountain,
And don't you see how violently water
Geysers beams and timbers? The deeper we shove them,
The harder we push them down, all might and main—
With just that energy water shoots them back,
Heaving them up till they leap clear into air.
Yet, I suppose, we have no doubt all things,
So far as in them lies, are carried down
Through empty space. So flames, through wafts of air,
Must rise, impelled, although their weight fights back
To bring them downward. Don't you see the torches
Of the night sky draw their long fiery trails
Wherever nature gives them passageway?
Don't you see stars and meteors fall to earth?
Even the sun from heaven's height rains heat,
Sows fields with light. From heaven to earth descends

Downward the course of heat. Watch lightning flash
Across the countering winds; now here, now there,
Dart the cloud-riving fires; most often, though,
The bolts drive down to earth.

                     I'd have you know
That while these particles come mostly down,
Straight down of their own weight through void, at times—
No one knows when or where—they swerve a little,
Not much, but just enough for us to say
They change direction. Were this not the case,
All things would fall straight down, like drops of rain,
Through utter void, no birth-shock would emerge
Out of collision, nothing be created.

If anyone thinks heavier bodies fall
More swiftly in their downward plunge, and thus
Fall on the lighter ones, and by this impact
Cause generation, he is very wrong.
To be sure, whatever falls through air or water
Goes faster in proportion to its weight,
For air's a frailer element than water.
Neither imposes quite the same delay
On all things passing through them, though both yield
More quickly to the heavier. But void
Can never hold up anything at all,
Never; its very essence is to yield.
So all things, though their weights may differ, drive
Through unresisting void at the same rate,
With the same speed. No heavier ones can catch
The lighter from above, nor downward strike
Such blows as might effect the variance
In motion nature gives to things. There must,
I emphasize, there has to be, a swerve
No more than minimal, for otherwise
We'd seem to predicate a slanting motion,
But this the facts refute. It's obvious,
It's clear to see, that substances don't sidle,

Fall sidewise, hurtling downward; but whose eyes
Are quick enough to see they never veer
With almost infinitesimal deviation?

If cause forever follows after cause
In infinite, undeviating sequence
And a new motion always has to come
Out of an old one, by fixed law; if atoms
Do not, by swerving, cause new moves which break
The laws of fate; if cause forever follows,
In infinite sequence, cause—where would we get
This free will that we have, wrested from fate,
By which we go ahead, each one of us,
Wherever our pleasures urge? Don't we also swerve
At no fixed time or place, but as our purpose
Directs us? There's no doubt each man's will
Initiates action, and this prompting stirs
Our limbs to movement. When the gates fly open,
No racehorse breaks as quickly as he wants to,
For the whole body of matter must be aroused,
Inspired to follow what the mind desires;
So, you can see, motion begins with will
Of heart or mind, and from that will moves on
Through all the framework. This is not the same
As our advance when we are prodded on
Or shoved along by someone else's force.
Under those circumstances, it is clear
That all our substance moves against our will,
Violence-driven, till our purpose checks it.
A foreign force often propels men on,
Makes them go forward, hurries them pell-mell.
Yet you see, don't you, something in ourselves
Can offer this force resistance, fight against it,
And this resistance has sufficient power
To permeate the body, to check the course,
To bring it to a halt? In atoms also
There has to be some other cause for motion
Beyond extrinsic thrust or native weight,

And this third force is resident in us
Since we know *nothing can be born of nothing.*
It is weight that stops all things from being caused
By blows, by outer force. Well then (you ask)
What keeps the mind from having inside itself
Some such compulsiveness in all its doings,
What keeps it from being matter's absolute slave?
The answer is, that our free-will derives
From just that ever-so-slight atomic swerve
At no fixed time, at no fixed place whatever.

Matter has never thickened or thinned; it cannot,
Since it has neither increase nor diminution.
Atoms are moving in the same way now
As they have done forever, and will do
Forever, and all things will come to birth
Just as they always have, will grow, will thrive
According to their nature's law; there lies
No place for matter of any kind whatever
To make escape to from its absolute sum,
And no place, either, whence new quantity
Could possibly come rushing in, to change
All nature, alter motion.

                            It's no wonder
That while the atoms are in constant motion,
Their total seems to be at total rest,
Save here and there some individual stir.
Their nature lies beyond our range of sense,
Far, far beyond. Since you can't get to see
The things themselves, they're bound to hide their moves,
Especially since things we *can* see, often
Conceal their movements, too, when at a distance.
Take grazing sheep on a hill, you know they move,
The woolly creatures, to crop the lovely grass
Wherever it may call each one, with dew
Still sparkling it with jewels, and the lambs,
Fed full, play little games, flash in the sunlight,

Yet all this, far away, is just a blur,
A whiteness resting on a hill of green.
Or when great armies sweep across great plains
In mimic warfare, and their shining goes
Up to the sky, and all the world around
Is brilliant with their bronze, and trampled earth
Trembles under the cadence of their tread,
While mountains echo the uproar to the stars,
The horsemen gallop and shake the very ground,
And yet high in the hills there is a place
From which the watcher sees a host at rest,
And only a brightness resting on the plain.

Now learn what kinds of matter constitute
These first-beginnings, and how different
They are in shape, how varied in their forms.
Many, indeed, are very much alike,
But, as a general rule, they tend to differ.
No wonder, either, for, as I have taught,
Their numbers are so great they have no end,
No possible sum; in such a multitude
They could not possibly be spun alike,
The same in warp and woof. Parade before you
The human race, the silent swimming creatures,
Wild beasts, tame cattle, all the varying birds
Flocking to river banks or lakes or springs
Or flying through the pathlessness of woods—
Go on from there, look close at every kind,
And you will find no two identical.
Otherwise, mothers would not know their young,
Nor young their mothers; but we see they do
And recognize each other, every bit
As well as human beings do. A calf,
Struck down before some god's august demesne,
Lies fallen near the incense-bearing altar,
The warm blood flowing from his breast. His mother,
Bereft, wanders in search through upland green,
Distinguishes this cloven print from that one,

Surveys all regions, hoping for a glimpse
Of her lost young one, fills the leafy groves
With plaintive lowing, comes to the stall again,
At a standstill in her heartbreak. Osiers, grass
Dew-fresh, streams running level with their banks,
Can hold no charm for her, nor turn her mood
Away from sorrow. It's no help at all
For her to look at others of her kind,
Young ones in happy romping over meadows.
She seeks her own, the one best known to her.
It's the same way with little bleating goats
Who know their long-horned mothers, or with lambs,
Those frisky little rascals, in the herds
Of sheep; each one, as nature tells him to,
Comes skippity-hop to his own proper milk-tap.
Or take an ear of corn; you will find no kernel
Exactly like another. No two shells
That decorate the margin of the shore
Where sea comes curving over thirsty sand
Are quite the same in whorl and convolution.
This has to be the way it is, this has to—
I say it over and over—be the way
With the most infinitesimal first-beginnings,
Turned out by nature, not by handiwork,
Not machine-tooled, always in one set mold,
But different from each other in their flying.

This makes it easy for us to explain
Why lightning's fire can penetrate more deeply
Than any torch-flame we on earth can manage.
You can say that lightning, heaven's fire, consists
Of smaller particles, more fine, and so
Can pass through pores which torch-fire, born of wood,
Could never enter. Light comes through a pane,
Water does not. Why so? It must be, light
Has smaller particles than those of water.
Wine flows more quickly through a colander
Than olive oil; the latter's elements

Are either coarser, or so hooked, so meshed
They can't so easily be pulled apart
And one by one ooze through in proper course.

Honey and milk are pleasant to the tongue,
But wormwood and red gentian both are bitter,
With a nasty taste that puckers up the mouth.
From smooth round atoms come those things which touch
Our senses pleasantly; what feels harsh, or rough,
Is held together by particles more barbed
And therefore seems to slash across our senses
Or by its entrance shatter and break.

                          All things
We feel to be agreeable clash with those
We deem unpleasant; they are unlike in shape.
Don't ever think the rasping of a saw
That sets your teeth on edge has elements
As smooth as those of a music, which the bards
Draw from the harpstrings where their fingers move.
Don't think that atoms of like form assail
Our nostrils when rotten carcasses are burning
As when the air is filled with eastern saffron
Or when the altars breathe Panchaian scent.
Don't think that lovely hues are ever born
From the same atoms as those that smart the eyes,
Force tears, and seem in general foul and ugly.
No sense-delighting object has been made
Without some elemental smoothness in it,
And, on the other hand, whatever seems
Noxious, disgusting, has, as its deep core,
The presence of rough matter. In between
Are things by no means absolutely smooth,
Yet not all barbs and hooks, but little spurs
Projecting just a bit, to tease our senses,
To tickle rather than sting, wine-lees, for instance,
Or elecampane. Warm fire, cold frost, are toothed
With different cogs; our human sense of touch

Gives evidence of that; by all that's holy
I swear, by touch alone men come to know
Sensations of the body, whether things
From outside enter it, or from within
Hurt issues, or the sweet release of love.
Sometimes within the body the atoms riot,
Reacting from some blow; their turbulence
Causes internal pain. See for yourself—
Strike part of your body with your hand; what happens?
So, first-beginnings must have different forms,
Each with a different effect.

                              Hard things,
Tight-knit, must have more barbs and hooks to hold them,
Must be more interwoven, like thorny branches
In a close hedgerow; in this class of things
We find, say, adamant, flint, iron, bronze
That shrieks in protest if you try to force
The stout oak door against the holding bars.
Fluid substance, though, must be composed
Of smooth and rounded particles. Poppy seeds
Might serve as an example, being round
And small and smooth, mercurial as drops
Of water, almost never held together—
And finally all elusive things that vanish
In moments from our sight, like smoke, flame, cloud,
If not made up of particles quite smooth,
Completely round, are still not too entangled,
Too interwoven, too close-meshed. They can
Pierce flesh, for instance, even penetrate rock.
This kind of object has to be composed
Of elements that are sharp, but not close-linked,
More like a flying dart than a roll of barbed wire.
Don't be surprised that fluid can be bitter
Like salt sea-brine, where smooth and round combine,
Yet mixed with them is something pitted, pocked,
Not necessarily hooked together, just rough
Enough to cause some trouble. There's a way

Of testing this: you can make salt water fresh
By filtering it through earth, and not just once,
But over and over again; what happens then
Is that the rougher parts are caught and held,
Catch on the earth, whereas the smoother ones
Come through all gentled, mild and sweet; they leave
Above them the foul brackish elements
Whose rougher surface helps them stick in earth.

This much explained, let me go on to state
A corollary truth that follows from it,
Namely, that atoms have a finite number
Of differing shapes. Were this not so, some seeds
Would have to be of infinite magnitude.
If you take one body, reasonably small,
There cannot be too many different forms
Inside it; let's suppose one chunk of matter
Consists of three much smaller parts, or maybe
Add a few more; when you take all these parts
Placing them high and low, or left and right,
When you have learned, by shifting them around,
Each possible arrangement, pattern, shape,
Then, if you seek still further variation,
You will have to add new parts, repeat the process
As long as you want the shapes to vary more.
It follows that out of increase of substance
Ensues variety of form. You must not,
Because of this, conclude that atoms are
Infinite in their possible number of shapes,
For this would force you to admit they were
Of infinite size. Impossible; I've proved it.
Ridiculous to assume a lack of limit,
Of mete and bound. Your foreign cloaks,
Your Meliboaen crimsons, deeply dyed
With color from the shells of Thessaly,
And all the peacock hues of all the world,
Whose graces, in gold sunlight, make us smile,
All these would fade to nothing, overcome

By new triumphant colors. Odors, too,
The scents of honey, of myrrh, would fade and die
And silence fall on the sweet sounds of music,
Swan-song, the harmony of voice and lyre,
With excellence forever giving way
To super-excellence. Things might also change
Not only for the better, but for worse,
Bad smells turn into stenches, ugly sights
Be veritable eyesores, and the taste
Gag at what's on the palate. But we know
This does not happen, proper bonds are set
To all things, so, perforce, we must admit
There must be limits to the range of forms
Matter can ever take. From fire to ice,
From ice to fire, the course is strictly set
Whichever way we go, though in between
Lie many stations intermediate,
Warm, luke-warm, tepid, chilly, cooler, cold,
But at each terminal the blaze of a sword-point
Confronts us, flaming hot, or glaring cold.

This much explained, let me go on again
To state a further corollary: atoms
Of similar shape are infinite in number.
The count of shapes, of forms, is limited,
Specimens, therefore, of any single form,
Must either be unlimited in number
Or matter's total sum have to be finite,—
But this I have proved is quite impossible.
My verse has shown how particles cohere,
How, from the infinite, the sum of things
Endures, impelled, in its eternal harness
By the ox-goad of forever.

                              It is true
Some animals appear to be more scarce,
Nature less fertile in them than in others,
But in some far-off land, some realm remote,
Thousands on thousands may fill out the tally.

Just as, of quadrupeds, we see the breed
Of elephants, those snaky-handed beasts
Whose native India a solid wall
Of ivory protects. This must have taken
The tusks of more than millions, yet we see
Only a very few of these huge creatures.
Still, for the sake of argument, let me grant
That there is one thing, single and unique,
With nothing like it in the whole wide world.
But how could this be given birth, or growth,
Or sustenance, without an infinite
Available supply of primal source?
Suppose the first-beginnings of this object
Were finite, countable, yet forever tossed
Through all the universe, what force, what pact
Could bring them so together in that sea,
That maelstrom of confusing otherness?
They'd have, I think, no possible scheme for union,
Are more like what you'd see on a vast ocean
After a terrible storm, and wrack and ruin
Where wind and wave break, toss beams, ribs, thwarts, yards,
Prows, masts, smashed oars, hurl figure-heads and stern-posts
Along the shores of every coast, in warning
To mortals: *Never trust the sea, whose might*
Is endless as her treachery; avoid her,
Do not believe her false seducing smile.
This illustration shows that once you make
The count of atoms limited, what follows
Is just this kind of tossing, being tossed,
Flotsam and jetsam through the seas of time,
Never allowed to join in peace, to dwell
In peace, estranged from amity and growth.
The lesson is plain as day, that things are born,
That things increase, and therefore there must be
An infinite supply of matter for them.

The ways of death can not prevail forever,
Entombing healthiness, nor can birth and growth
Forever keep created things alive.

There is always this great elemental deadlock,
This warfare through all time. The keen for the dead
Blends with the cry that new-born babies raise
At their first shock by the light. Night follows day,
Dawn follows eventide, and never a one
That has not heard these feeble pulings sound
Through the more dark and somber threnodies.

It is well to nail this down, to keep in mind
This principle as well: that nature has
Nothing consisting of one element
And one alone, but everything is made
Of many elements combined together.
Whatever thing possesses many powers,
Many capacities, it thereby shows
It must contain so many kinds of atoms,
All sorts of different elements and shapes.
Earth, for example, holds those primal forms
From which her cooling sources roll, renew
Unbounded ocean; the same earth contains
The origins of fire, the burning deserts,
Volcanic Etnas; and again, she holds
The shining harvests, orchard loveliness,
Not only gifts for mortals, but the streams,
The leaves, the berries, for the animals
Roaming the mountains. Therefore she is called
The gods' Great Mother, Dam of all the Beasts,
Only Creatress of the race of men.

The old and learned poets of the Greeks
Have sung her praise—how, from her shrine, she comes
Riding in state, driving her lion-team,
Wherefrom we learn the great world hangs in air,
Land being unable to rest on land. The lions
In harness prove parental gentleness
Can tame the wildest creatures. On her head
She wears the mural crown; thus fortified,
Her heights sustain great cities. Borne aloft,

Her image, thus adorned, awes mighty lands
In her divine processional. Her name
Is, *The Idaean Mother;* many tribes
Have called her so from ancient times. They gave her
A Phrygian retinue because, they say,
Out of that realm, spreading across the world,
Came wheat and corn. They give her eunuch priests
To demonstrate that men are sometimes found
Unworthy of their fathers, ravishers
Of the maternal godhead, and such men
Must not send offspring to the shores of light.
Their open palms slap the taut bongo-drums
To terrible thunder, the hollow cymbals clash,
The horns blare raucous, and the flutes pipe shrill
With sharp insistence; there are spears and swords
In violence brandished, so that wicked hearts,
Ungrateful spirits of the mob, are cowed
Before her great divinity. And so,
When she is borne, all silent, through great towns,
Bestowing her unspoken blessing there,
Men strew her way with silver and with bronze,
Lavish in giving, and rose-petals fall
Like snow, to form a canopy of shade
Over The Mother, and her retinue.
Next an armed band, whom the Greeks call Curetes,
Leap bloodstained in a war dance. The stamp, the beat,
Make the crests nod with the terrible jerking heads.
They remind us of the storied ones in Crete
Who hid the crying of the infant Jove
Under their uproar, boys around a boy
Swift dancing, clashing arms in shock and beat
So father Saturn could not catch and eat him
Wounding his mother's heart. So armed men now
Give the Great Mother escort, and these arms
May signify that the goddess orders men
To have an active will for the defense
Of their own country with the arms of valor,
To be the pride and glory of their fathers.

All this, all this is wonderfully told,
A marvel of tradition, and yet far
From the real truth. Reject it—for the gods
Must, by their nature, take delight in peace,
Forever calm, serene, forever far
From our affairs, beyond all pain, beyond
All danger, in their own resources strong,
Having no need of us at all, above
Wrath or propitiation.

                              Let a man
Call upon Neptune, if he likes, say Ceres
When he means corn or wheat, miscall his wine
By an apostrophe to Father Bacchus,
Let him keep on repeating that our globe
Is the gods' mother—but let him, all this while,
Be careful, really, not to let religion
Infect, pollute, corrupt him. Earth indeed
Is quite insentient, has always been,
And as possessor of all particles
Sends many forth in many ways to light,
No consciousness about it.

                              A single field
Often has in it wooly grazing sheep,
The warlike breed of horses, the horned cattle,
All under the same canopy of heaven,
All drinking from one river. So they live,
Each in its fashion; each perpetuates
Ancestral archetypes, ways of behavior.
In every kind of grass and grain and stream
Diverse abundance must exist, to feed
Each different demand. And every beast
Consists of bones, blood, veins, warmth, fluid, flesh,
Sinews, and so on—very different things
Composed of atoms differently shaped.
And things burnt in a fire—whatever else
They have, or lack, in common—share, at least,

Variety in their issue, embers, sparks,
Light, flying ash. Range wide and far, you'll find
The scheme consistent; everything conceals
Within its single substance many a mote,
Many a particle, all different.
Some visible objects have not only hue
But color and taste. Our gifts are great in number
And manifold in form. Odors can reach
Where hues are barred, colors can penetrate
Where taste cannot, and so on. We conclude
From this that in their basic elements
There must be difference of shape. One mass
Is formed from many differing particles.

In what I write here, common elements
And different ones run through the words and lines.
This is not to say that the same letter's found
In every word; it might be possible
For the same letters to fashion different words,
Like *verse* and *sever*, say. This principle
Applies in other areas as well.
Some elements are common to many things
But they can differ in the whole effect,
As happens with the human race and trees,
With animals and crops.

                              You must not think
That all things can combine in every way,
Every conceivable pattern, for, if so,
You'd see such freaks as men-half-beasts, and boughs,
Instead of arms and legs, coming from torsos.
You'd see marine-terrestrial animals,
Chimaeras, for example, breathing fire
Out of their ugly faces, browsing over
All-mothering earth; but it is plain as day
This does not happen, since we see all things
Maintain the proper order of their kind,
Same kind of parenthood, same kind of seed,

Definite causes, definite effects,
A fixed, assured procedure. In all things
The sustenance they take prevades the limbs,
The particles of nourishment combine
To set those limbs in motion. We can see
The opposite of this process also,—nature
Often casts out improper elements,
Rejects them; many elements are driven
Outward as if by blows, they cannot join
Within this frame, or that, can neither feel
Nor even feign the attributes of life.
Not only animals obey these laws,
The code applies to everything. As all
Are different, so, in their origin
They must derive from different shapes. Of course
I do not say that nothing ever looks
Like anything else, but that in general
Species are different, from different seed,
With different intervals, junctions, ways—weight, force,
Motion, and so on. Not animals alone
Are separate and distinct, one from the other,
But also land and sea, heaven and earth.

There is more to learn; for me it's pleasant work.
Do listen—I don't want you to suppose
White atoms form those white things that you see
Before your eyes, or that black objects come
From particles of black. Never believe
That any visible color is derived
From motes that color. Basic elements
Simply do not have color, none at all,
In that respect being neither like nor unlike
The larger forms they fashion. You'd be wrong
To think imagination can't conceive
Of objects lacking color. Those born blind,
Who never have seen the sunlight, learn by touch
The sense of bodies, though ideas of color
Mean nothing to them, and the color-concept
Is by no means an absolute. You and I

Know this from our experience; have we not
In utter darkness put our hands on things
Without the least idea what color they were?
Well, then: if anything can be colorless,
Atoms must be such things. Here is the proof:
Each color can be changed to any other,
But basic elements should not act like this.
Something must stand immutable, it must,
Lest all things be reduced to absolute nothing.
If anything is changed, leaving its bounds,
That is the death of what it was before.
So don't go dyeing atoms any color,
Or you'll have everything annihilated.

All right, then: first-beginnings have no color,
But they do differ in shape, and from this cause
Arise effects of color variation.
It makes a world of difference in what order
They form their combinations, how they are held,
How give, take, interact. For an example,
Things black a little while ago turn white,
All shining white, as a dark sea can change
From sullen black to the shine of dancing marble
When the great winds go sweeping over the waves.
You can say that what we often see as black,
When its matter gets disturbed, or its order shifts
With something added, something taken away,
Looks, almost in a moment, white and shining.
But if the ocean-surface were composed
Of blue-green atoms, it could never whiten.
Mix blue in as you like, stir it around,
You won't get white. But if these ocean-atoms
That give the sea its single perfect luster
Were every kind of color, the way a square
Is formed, or can be, out of triangles
Trapezoids, rhombs, and so on, which we see
Within those four right angles, even so
In the pure perfect luster, we should note
All sorts of different colors. Furthermore,

There is nothing in geometry to keep
Forms of a different kind from adding up
To squares, but a variety of hues
Can't possibly fuse to a single color.

It's a delusion, but a tempting one
To assign color to the primal motes,
But this is error. White can't come from white,
Nor black from black, but both of them can come
From different hues; white will arise, for instance,
Much sooner out of never-a-color-at-all
Than it ever will from black, or any hue
That contradicts and fights it.

                                        Furthermore,
Since, without light, color cannot exist,
And since the atoms never reach the light,
They must be colorless. In the blind dark
What color could they have? Even in bright day
Hues change as light-fall comes direct or slanting.
The plumage of a dove, at nape or throat,
Seems in the sunlight sometimes ruby-red
And sometimes emerald-green suffused with coral.
A peacock's tail, in the full blaze of light,
Changes in color as he moves and turns.
Since the light's impact causes this, we know
Color depends on light. Our eyes receive
One kind of impulse when they look at white
And quite another from black, but the sense of touch
Cares nothing at all for colors, only for shapes,
So first-beginnings have no need of color,
But from their varied forms derive their force,
Their identifying impact.

                            Now, if we say
No single shape has one consistent hue,
But any shape can come in any color,

Why aren't the things they form likewise imbued
With every possible rainbow variation?
Your flying crows might any minute shed
White plumes, or swans come black out of black eggs,
And everything be colored every which way.

Reduce a thing, divide it, strip it down,
And you can watch its color disappear.
Pull a red cloth to pieces, thread by thread,
And all its scarlet fades; from this we know
Parts, in the process of becoming smaller,
Have lost all color by the time they reach
The level of the atom.

                    Finally,
Since not all substances, as you admit,
Produce either sound or smell, you are correct
To argue these are attributes they lack.
By the same token, things we cannot see
Are just as sure to be devoid of color
As they are free from having sound or smell,
And a quick intellect can recognize
Things can exist without these attributes,
As without certain others.

                    Don't suppose
It is only color that the atoms lack.
They are devoid of warmth, of heat, of cold;
They are soundless, sapless; as they move along
They leave no trail of scent. You know what happens
When you prepare to compound some perfume
Of marjoram and myrrh and fragrant nard.
One of the first things that you have to take,
With just as little odor as possible,
Is olive-oil for a base, because its scent
Won't interfere or dominate the blend
Concocted in its blandness. So the atoms
Impart to things they bring to birth no smell,

No sound—they've no such residues to spare—
No taste, no sense of hot or cold; all these
Ephemerals are mortal, pliant, soft,
Brittle, or hollow; no such properties
Ever inhere in atoms, or we'd lack
The indestructible solid base we need
Lest all things be reduced to utter nothing.

Things which we see are sentient, we must now
Acknowledge, have their origin in things
Quite without sentience. Many things we know
Neither refute this nor give argument
Of any force against it, but they tend
Rather to give it credence and support.
They lead us by the hand, almost, to show
That animals are born from senseless stuff.
Haven't you seen live worms come crawling out
From a manure pile, after heavy rain
Has drenched earth rotten? The same thing occurs
In the same way with all the other things:
Rivers and leaves and forage are transformed
To animals, and animals to men
And our own bodies oftentimes sustain
The strength of predatory beasts and birds.
Nature turns all the foods to living flesh
And out of this creates all sentient things;
In the same way she makes dry tinder break
In flame, thus turning everything to fire.
The most important point—I hope you see this—
Consists in the arrangement of the atoms,
Their order, their reciprocal give and take.

Now what's all this that shakes and moves your mind,
Turns your perceptions hither and yon, forbids
Acceptance of belief that sentient things
Are born, or may be, out of things insentient?
Stones, wood, earth, all of them combined, can never
Produce a living sense, but bear in mind

I do not say that consciousness derives
All helter-skelter from all creative force,
From all the elements that make up matter.
I do insist that we must recognize
How small the primal atoms are that make
A sentient object, I insist again
That we must know their order, shape, design.
In wood, in clods, we see them not at all,
Yet, when the rain rots wood and crumbles clod,
The little worms are born. The reason is
That a new cause, in this case rain, has broken
The old arrangement, so disturbed the atoms,
That new things have been brought to birth, and must be.
Now, those who argue sentient things are formed
From other sentient things, and these derive
From others still, would have to claim that atoms
Are somehow soft, and therefore must be mortal.
Sensation, as we know, inheres in things
Like sinews, bowels, veins, and all of these
Consist of soft and perishable stuff.
Well, even so,—suppose such particles
Are everlasting, they would have to have
The feelings proper to one part alone
Or else be thought, each by itself, to be
The likeness of a fully sentient creature.
But parts can't have sensation by themselves,
They are dependent, rather, on each other.
Does a hand feel hand-like, or have any feeling
When severed from the body? Why, of course not!
So that takes care of half of that dilemma,
Leaving us to conclude that atoms must
Be like ourselves, to feel the selfsame things
That we do, share with us the sense of life.
But then how can we call them first-beginnings
Or primal motes, exempt from ways of death,
If they are living creatures, and, as such,
Mortal by definition? Resolve the paradox,
Concede them immortality: what then?

They'll join, they'll meet, they'll reproduce themselves,
Bring nothing forth except a beastly mob,
A common herd, as men and cattle do,
Or wilder animals. If, by chance, they lose
One bodily sensation and gain another,
What good the loss, the gain? We must resort
To the old argument: as eggs become
Chickens, as worms emerge from rotten earth
After a heavy rain, so sentience must
Be born out of insentience.

                              Somebody now
Will argue that sensation can arise
From non-sensation; all it takes is change,
Something like birth, some such creative process.
The way to answer this is to make clear,
To prove, that birth and change of any kind
Alike depend upon the prior force
Of an—I'd almost say—deliberate union.

You just can't have sensation in a body
Before its creature's born, while all its matter,
The elements of its make-up, are dispersed
All over the world, in river, air, and earth,
As well as earth's created growing things,
And have not come together, in a way
Suited to movement, brought to light and life
The all-perceiving, all-protective sense.

Sometimes some heavier blow than natural
Strikes down some living thing, confusing all
Its senses, whether of body or of mind.
Because of this, the arrangements of the atoms
Are sundered, all the vital movements blocked,
Until the shock, diffused through all the limbs,
Loosens the bonds of spirit from body, sends
That spirit, shattered and fragmented, forth
From every portal. What else can a blow

Succeed in doing, except shatter and break?
Sometimes less violent blows are struck, and then
The vital forces win, they win, they quell
The riots, they recall to normal ways,
Expel the dominance of the tyrant death
From lording it over the body, light again
The fires of sense, almost gone out. How else
Can consciousness come back from the very door
Of death, reverse its almost-finished journey?

Since pain exists when violence attacks
Material particles within the body,
Shaking them loose, troubling their residence
In flesh and bone, but, once they settle down
In peace again, a calm delight ensues—
From this we know that atoms cannot ache
With any pain or grief, cannot rejoice
With pleasure, since they have no elements
To be disturbed, upset, or be restored
To profitable sweetness. They must be,
It has to follow, quite sensationless.

All animals have feelings, that we know
But still, it makes no sense that every mote,
Every particular atom in their make-up
Has, in its essence, the same kind of feeling.
As for the human race, well, what about it?
Do those peculiar atoms, out of which
We are compounded, shake their sides with mirth,
Bedew their cheeks with tears? Are they smart enough
To talk about the way things mix together?
Do they investigate their own beginnings?
If they're composed of other elements,
And those of others still, and so on, and so on,
There's just no place where you can dare to stop.
As long as you keep saying that a thing
Is talking, laughing, being wise, I'll hound you
Until you stop insisting things are made

Of particles like themselves. That's foolishness,
Sheer lunacy. Surely, a man can laugh
And not be made of laughing particles;
He can be wise, talk sense, and reason well
Without one philosophical atom in him.
It is only proper, then, to realize
That every sentient creature which we see
Is made of particles with no sensation.

We all have come from heavenly seed; we all
Have the same father, and our mother earth
Receives from him the fertilizing showers.
So pregnant, she brings forth the shining grain,
The trees that make us glad, the race of men,
The generations of wild beasts, the food
By which they feed, increase and multiply.
She is rightly called our mother, and the sons
Of earth return to earth, but any part
Sent down from heaven, must ascend again
Recalled to the high temples of the sky.
And death does not destroy the elements
Of matter, only breaks their combinations,
Joins them again in other ways, to cause
Changes of form and color, to bestow
Consciousness, or withdraw it in a moment.
It makes a world of difference in what order
Atoms form combinations, how they are held,
And how they move together. Do not think
They hold forever in their keeping things
Which in our sight float over surfaces,
Are born, meet sudden death. In my own verse
It makes a difference in what ways I set
My words, my parts of speech. No two may be
Alike exactly, but they share alike
Many a letter common to them both.
The order makes the difference. So it is
With more material objects: change the order,

Motion, position, combination, shape,
And all will have to change.

                    Direct your mind
To a true system. Here is something new
For ear and eye. Nothing is ever so easy
But what, at first, it is difficult to trust.
Nothing is great and marvelous, but what
All men, a little at a time, begin
To mitigate their sense of awe. Look up,
Look up at the pure bright color of the sky,
The wheeling stars, the moon, the shining sun!
If all these, all of a sudden, should arise
For the first time before our mortal sight,
What could be called more wonderful, more beyond
The heights to which aspiring mind might dare?
Nothing, I think. And yet, a sight like this,
Marvelous as it is, now draws no man
To lift his gaze to heaven's bright areas.
We are a jaded lot. But even so
Don't be too shocked by something new, too scared
To use your reasoning sense, to weigh and balance,
So that if in the end a thing seems true,
You welcome it with open arms; if false,
You do your very best to strike it down.
The sum of space is infinite, reaching far
Beyond the ramparts of the world; the mind
Persists in questioning: what can be there?
What is there so far off, toward which the urge
Of the free spirit flies?

                    There is no end,
No limit to the cosmos, above, below,
Around, about, stretching on every side.
This I have proven, but the fact itself
Cries loud in proclamation, nature's deep
Is luminous with proof. The universe

Is infinitely wide; its vastness holds
Innumerable seeds, beyond all count,
Beyond all possibility of number,
Flying along their everlasting ways.
So it must be unthinkable that our sky
And our round world are precious and unique
While all those other motes of matter flit
In idleness, achieve, accomplish nothing,
Especially since this world of ours was made
By natural process, as the atoms came
Together, willy-nilly, quite by chance,
Quite casually and quite intentionless
Knocking against each other, massed, or spaced
So as to colander others through, and cause
Such combinations and conglomerates
As form the origin of mighty things,
Earth, sea and sky, and animals and men.
Face up to this, acknowledge it. I tell you
Over and over—out beyond our world
There are, elsewhere, other assemblages
Of matter, making other worlds. Oh, ours
Is not the only one in air's embrace.

With infinite matter available, infinite space,
And infinite lack of any interference,
Things certainly ought to happen. If we have
More seeds, right now, than any man can count,
More than all men of all time past could reckon,
And if we have, in nature, the same power
To cast them anywhere at all, as once
They were cast here together, let's admit—
We really have to—there are other worlds,
More than one race of men, and many kinds
Of animal generations.

                    Furthermore,
Adding up all the sum, you'll never find
One single thing completely different

From all the rest, alone, apart, unique,
Sole product, single specimen of its kind.

Look at the animals: is this not true
Of mountain-ranging species, and of men,
Of the silent schools of fish, of flying things?
Likewise you must admit that earth, sun, moon,
Ocean, and all the rest, are not unique,
But beyond reckoning or estimate.
Their term of life is definitely set
And so remains, their substance is of stuff
No less ephemeral than what we see
In the teeming multitudes of our own earth.

Holding this knowledge, you can't help but see
That nature has no tyrants over her,
But always acts of her own will; she has
No part of any godhead whatsoever.
By all that's holy in the tranquil calm
Where the gods pass serene eternal days
I ask you—which of them is strong enough
To rule the sum of things, to hold the reins
Of absolute profundity, or move the skies
To turn together? Who can warm the lands
To fruitfulness with fire sent down from heaven?
Who can be immanent in every time,
In every place—to cloud the world in dark,
To shake the quiet areas of sky
With terrible sound? Who sends the lightning's blast
Even at his own temples? Who departs
To wilderness, but as he goes, in wrath,
Lets fly the bolts that pass the guilty by
And murder undeserving innocents?

Now since the origin of all the world,
The birthday of the sea and earth and sky,
Many additional particles have come
From outwardness, and many, many seeds

Combined by the tossing of the mighty all,
All this, that lands and oceans might increase,
The mansion of the heaven widen, lift
Its high abodes above the earth, and air
Go swirling upward, for all bodies are
Distributed by impact, each assigned
From everywhere to its own place; fire goes
To fire, and earth to earth, and air to air,
Moisture to moisture, till that final time
When growth is no more possible, the end
Which nature, maker of all things, has given.
This happens when the vital tides have turned
From flow to ebb; all things are bound to halt,
To age, as nature checks her own increase.
It works like this—whatever growing things
You see rejoicing, swelling out, in pride
Ascending, as it were, the stairs of life,
These are attracting to themselves more stuff
Than they let go of; food and sustenance
Come easily to the veins, and pores are kept
Tight-closed enough to stop the seep of age.
There is always diminution, ebb, retreat,
But for a while our gain exceeds our loss
Until we reach that highest point of ripeness.
From there we go, a little at a time,
Downhill; age breaks our oak, dissolves our strength
To watery feebleness. It's the solemn truth
That when their growth has ended, greater things,
The larger, wider, more heroic, stand
The more susceptible; their measure proves
Too difficult for nourishment, they need
More than they can receive of sustenance,
Being such lavish givers. It is food
That every creature needs, the food that mends,
Supports, renews, replenishes, but now
Nature can give no more, and income must
Be less than outgo. So things wither, die,
Made mean by loss, by blows, within, without,

Assailed, beseiged, betrayed, till at long last
Food fails, and the great walls are battered in.
In just this way the ramparts of the world,
For all their might, will some day face assault,
Be stormed, collapse in ruin and in dust.
It is happening already; our poor earth,
Worn out, exhausted, brings to birth no more
Great eons, Titans, huge majestic beasts,
Only our own disgusting little days,
Midges and gnats. I can't believe that men
Swung down from heaven on a golden chain,
Sprang from the sea or the rock-pounding waves,
But the same earth who nourishes them now
Once brought them forth, and gave them, to their joy,
Vineyards and shining harvests, pastures, arbors,
And all this now our very utmost toil
Can hardly care for, we wear down our strength
Whether in oxen or in men, we dull
The edges of our ploughshares, and in return
Our fields turn mean and stingy, underfed,
And so today the farmer shakes his head,
More and more often sighing that his work,
The labor of his hands, has come to naught.
When he compares the present to the past,
The past was better, infinitely so,
His father's lot was fortunate, his world
So filled with dedication that it gave
Great ease of life in narrow boundaries,
When no man held a vast estate—but now
The gloomy cultivator of the vine,
Degenerate and wilted, wearies heaven
With petulant complaining, fails to see
That all things, little by little, waste away
As time's erosion crumbles them to doom.

# *Book* III

O glory of the Greeks, the first to raise
The shining light out of tremendous dark
Illumining the blessings of our life,
You are the one I follow; in your steps
I tread, not as a rival, but for love
Of your example. Does the swallow vie
With swans? Do wobbly-legged little goats
Compete in strength and speed with thoroughbreds?
You, father, found the truth; you gave to us
A father's wisdom, and from every page,
O most illustrious in renown, we take,
As bees do from the flowery banks of summer,
The benefit of all your golden words,
The gold most worthy of eternal life;
For, once your reason, your divining sense,
Begins its proclamation, telling us
The way things are, all terrors of the mind
Vanish, are gone; the barriers of the world
Dissolve before me, and I see things happen
All through the void of empty space. I see
The gods majestic, and their calm abodes
Winds do not shake, nor clouds befoul, nor snow
Violate with the knives of sleet and cold;
But there the sky is purest blue, the air
Is almost laughter in that radiance,
And nature satisfies their every need,
And nothing, nothing, mars their calm of mind.
No realms of Hell are ever visible,
But earth affords a view of everything,
Below and outward, all through space. I feel

A more than mortal pleasure in all this,
Almost a shudder, since your power has given
This revelation of all nature's ways.

Since I have taught how everything begins,
The nature of those first particles, their shape,
Their differences, their voluntary course,
Their everlasting motion, and the ways
Things are created from them, I must now
Make use of poetry to clarify
The nature of intelligence and spirit,
Of mind and soul. The fear of Acheron
Must, first and foremost, be dismissed; this fear
Troubles the life of man from its lowest depths,
Stains everything with death's black darkness, leaves
No pleasure pure and clear; it drives a man
To violate honor, or to break the bonds
Of friendship, and, in general, overthrow
All of the decencies. Men have betrayed
Their country or their parents, desperate
To avoid the realms of Acheron. I know—
Indeed I know—how people often say
That lives diseased, or lives of infamy
Are worse than any hell; they know the soul
Is made of blood, or air; they do not need
Our philosophical scheme. You recognize
All this as nothing but rank swagger, spoken
For self-assurance, not in true belief.
If these same men are banished from their land,
Exiled beyond the sight of men, defamed
By most disgraceful accusation, cursed
With every possible torment, still they live,
Keep living on; and everywhere they go,
Poor wretched outcasts, still they sacrifice:
They slay black cattle, they send offerings
Down to the shades below, direct their minds—
O much more zealously!—in bitter times
Religionward. If you would like to know

What a man really is, the time to learn
Comes when he stands in danger or in doubt.

That's when the words of truth come from his heart,
The mask is torn aside, reality
Remains for all to see. But avarice
And blind desire for honors urge men on
To trespass on the areas which the law
Forbids them, and they struggle night and day
As criminal accomplices to win
Toward heights of wealth—such vital wounds as these
Are aggravated by the fear of death.
Men seem to think that bitter poverty
And the contempt a low position brings
Are far from sweet and reassuring life,
Are hangers-on around the doors of death.
So a false panic harries them; they long
Too late for flight, for far-off distances;
Seek, through the blood of fellow-citizens,
A way to prosper; they amass estates
In avarice, pile one murder on another,
Rejoice when a brother dies, and hate and fear
The table of a kindly relative.
In the same way compulsive envy, born
Of the same fear, can make them waste away
Seeing a man blest with renown or power
Before their very eyes, while they are held,
Or so they mutter, in darkness and in muck.
Some die for lack of statues or a name;
It goes so far, sometimes, that fear of death
Induces hate of life and light, and men
Are so depressed that they destroy themselves
Having forgotten that this very fear
Was the first source and cause of all their woe.
As children tremble and fear everything
In the dark shadows, we, in the full light,
Fear things that really are not one bit more awful
That what poor babies shudder at in darkness,

The horrors they imagine to be coming.
Our terrors and our darknesses of mind
Must be dispelled then, not by sunshine's rays,
Not by those shining arrows of the light,
But by insight into nature, and a scheme
Of systematic contemplation.

                              First,
The mind—the intellect, we sometimes call it—
The force that gives direction to a life
As well as understanding, is a part
Of a man's make-up, every bit as much
As are his hands and feet and seeing eyes.
Some say the sentient mind is not located
In any one fixed area, but pervades
The body as a vital force; the Greeks
Called this a *harmony*, a relationship
Which gives us intellect, though mind itself
Lacks any fixed location. Just as health
Inheres in bodily structure, but no man
Has any part he can identify
As being the organ where his health resides,
So these philosophers give no fixed part
As the abode of mind. In this, I think,
They are very wrong indeed. Sometimes we see
Part of a body sicken before our eyes,
While what we do not see enjoys good health;
And it can be the other way around:
You can be sick in mind and well in body,
Your foot can hurt while you are free of headache.
When all our limbs relax in easy slumber
And our body lies insensible, unconscious,
There is something in us, wakeful even then,
Susceptible to anxiety or joy.
Look at what happens if some bodily parts,
More than a few, are lost, life still keeps on
Within the limbs; from this you can be sure
Sensation, sentience, dwells within the limbs

Without the need of common *harmony*
To be their source of consciousness. Again,
When a few particles of heat disperse
And breath is forced out of the mouth, the spirit
With that same breath leaves artery and bone.
Not all the organs, you must realize,
Are equally important nor does health
Depend on all alike, but there are some—
The seeds of breathing, warm vitality—
Whereby we are kept alive; when these are gone
Life leaves our dying members. So, since mind
And spirit are by nature part of man,
Let the musicians keep that term brought down
To them from lofty Helicon—or maybe
They found it somewhere else, made it apply
To something thitherto nameless in their craft—
I speak of *harmony*. Whatever it is,
Give it back to the musicians.

                              Now pay heed,
I have more to say. To start with, I maintain
That mind and spirit are held close together,
Compose one unity, but the lord and master
Holding dominion over all the body
Is purpose, understanding—in our terms
Mind or intelligence, and this resides
In the region of the heart. Hence we derive
Terror and fear and panic and delight.
Here therefore dwell intelligence and mind.
The rest of spirit is dispersed all through
The entire frame, and it obeys the mind,
Moves, gains momentum, at its nod and beck,
And mind alone is sensible or wise
Or glad all by itself, when body and soul
Are quite unmoved by anything; and as an eye
Or head can hurt us, though we feel no pain
In any other part, so now and then
The mind can suffer or rejoice, while spirit

Is nowhere stirred in any part by strangeness;
But when the mind is deeply moved by fear
We see the spirit share that panic sense
All through the body: sweat breaks out, and pallor comes;
The tongue grows thick, the voice is choked, the eyes
Grow dark, ears ring, the limbs collapse. Men faint,
We have often seen, from a terror in the mind;
From this example all can recognize
That spirit and mind are closely bound together,
And spirit, struck by the impulse of the mind,
Propels and thrusts the body.

                    This same doctrine
Shows that the nature of both mind and spirit
Must be corporeal. We are bound to admit
That spirit and mind are properties of body
When they propel the limbs, arouse from sleep,
Change an expression, turn a man around,
Control him utterly, but none of this
Is possible without contact, nor is touch
Possible without body. Furthermore,
You see that mind can sympathize with body,
Share its emotions. If a weapon drives
Deep into bone and sinew, and yet fails
To shatter life entirely, still it brings
Weakness, collapse, and turbulence of mind
Within the fallen victim, a desire,
Half-hearted and confused, to rise again.
So mind, which suffers under wounds and blows,
Must have a bodily nature.

                      I'll explain,
At this point, what that body's like, what forms it:
First, it is very delicate indeed,
Made of the most diminutive particles.
That this is so requires no argument
Beyond the fact that nothing seems to move
With such velocity as mind intends

Or mind anticipates; mind acts, we know,
Quicker than anything natural we see.
But anything so mobile must consist
Of particles very round and smooth indeed,
And very small indeed, to be so stirred,
So set in motion by the slightest urge.
Water is moved in just this way, and flows
With almost no impulsion, being formed
Of tiny little round motes, adaptable
Most easily for rolling. Honey, though,
Is more cohesive, less disposed to flow,
More sluggish, for its whole supply of matter
Is more condensed; its motes are not as smooth,
As round, as delicate. The slightest stir
Of air disturbs a cone of poppy seeds,
Sends the top sliding downward; no such breath
Is adequate to disturb a pile of pebbles
Or even a heap of wheat-ears. Bodies move
With speed proportionate to their size and weight,
If small, then swift. The heavy or the rough
Are the more stable, solid, hard to move.
Now, since the nature of the mind appears
Mobile, extremely so, it must consist
Of particles which are small and smooth and round.
This knowledge, my good scholar, you will find
To your advantage in more ways than one.
Another fact gives evidence how frail,
How delicate spirit is, or soul, or mind,
How almost infinitesimal its compass
Even supposing it were massed together:
When death's calm reassurance takes a man,
And mind and spirit have left him, you perceive
Nothing at all subtracted from the body,
Nothing of weight, of semblance, gone. Death shows
All that was his except the vital sense,
The warming breath. And so the spirit must
Consist throughout of very tiny seeds,
All sown minutely in sinew, flesh, and veins—

So tenuous that when it leaves the body
There seems no difference, no diminution
Of outward contour nor of inward weight.
The same thing happens when the scent of wine,
Or nard's aroma, or any effluence,
Vanishes into air, and still its source
Appears no less substantial to our eyes,
Especially since nothing of its weight
Is lost—so many and such tiny seeds
Imparting scent and flavor in all things.
Let me repeat: infinitesimal motes
Must form both mind and spirit, since we see
No loss of weight when these depart the body.

But do not think theirs is a simple nature.
A thin breath, mixed with heat, deserts the dying,
And this heat draws air with it; heat includes,
Because it is by nature rarefied,
Always an element of air. So now we find
The nature of the mind to be composite,
Threefold at least. But these are not enough
To cause sensation—reason would deny
That any one, or all, could generate
Sense-bringing movements or the stir of thought.
There must be a fourth element, and this
Lacks, so far, even a name; nothing exists
More tenuous, more mobile; it is made
Out of the smallest, lightest particles,
And it is this which first imparts to limbs
Sense-bringing movements. Being so minute,
It is most easily responsive, stirs
First into motion; heat is next, then wind
With its blind power, then air, then all things move.
The blood is roused, the vital organs feel
Sensation, even the marrow of the bones
Reacts to pleasure or its opposite.
Pain cannot penetrate too far, or evil
Seep its corrosive acid through the frame

Without so much disturbance and distress
That life has little room, and the motes of spirit
Fly every which way through the body's pores;
But as a rule this panic rush subsides
At the last moment, at the borderline,
And we stay strong enough to keep on living.

The poverty of our speech, our native tongue,
Makes it hard for me to say exactly how
These basic elements mingle, how they thrive
Once they have been arranged; but let me try
As best I can. To start with, all these motes
So move, so weave, so rush among each other
They can't be isolated, and no one
Could act if separated from the rest,
But the many, as it were, compose one mass,
One single entity. As any creature
Has scent, and heat, and taste, but from all these
A single separate physical bulk is grown,
So heat and air and wind's blind power combine
To form one nature, and that moving force
Which stirs them into action, spreads through flesh
The capability of sense. Deep down
This quality lies hidden, very deep,
So deep that nothing in us can be found
Below the spirit's spirit. In our limbs,
In all our substance, mind and spirit join
Their hidden forces, and are quite unseen,
Being formed of small and none too many motes,
So this fourth nameless element, though it hides
In the minutest motes, is lord of all,
Rules body and mind. Yet wind and heat and air
Must also act in concert, or combine
In rise and subsidence, reciprocal
In such a way that they continue one
In unity; otherwise the heat, the wind,
The power of air might scatter, torn apart,
To dissipate the principle of sense.

The mind in wrath makes use of heat—we talk
Of boiling anger or of blazing eyes;
And mind can know the icy chill of fear,
The shivering convulsion of the limbs,
While cattle seem by nature more inclined
To live in airs of calm, are seldom roused
By anger's torch, the reek of smoky shade,
Nor are they frozen by cold shafts of terror.
They have their places between deer and lions.
So with the race of man. Many are smoothed,
Polished by culture, seem alike, almost,
Yet the original character abides.
Don't ever think our evil ways can be
Entirely rooted out, so that one man
Will never tear at downhill speed to wrath,
Another be too cowardly, a third
Far too long-suffering, very much too calm
In taking insult. What a platitude
To say men differ in nature and behavior!
I cannot, here and now, bring forth to light
All the dark causes, or supply a list
Of names to identify this catalogue.
This much I think I can, and do, assert:
That our perverse vestigial native ways
Are small enough for reason to dispel
So that it lies within our power to live
Lives worthy of the gods.

                              This spirit, then,
Inheres in every body. It is both
The cause of health and guardian of the body.
These cling together, body and health, they have
Their roots in common, can't be torn asunder
Without annihilation. Can you take
The scent from balsam? It is just as hard
To sever mind and spirit from the body
Without complete and utter dissolution.
From the beginning all the elements

Are ever so tightly meshed and interwoven
Within their residence, and neither one
Can feel without the other's help. Their union,
Their common motions, are our source of feeling.
No body ever is born or ever grows
Out of itself alone, nor after death
Seems to endure. The body is not like water
Which gives off steam when heated, but remains
Intact itself; it is not this way with spirit
Whose going the abandoned framework might
Endure, survive—by no means. Body would die,
Be shattered, rot, without the spirit. So,
From life's conception, body and soul possess,
Even in the womb, a kind of inter-touch
From which they come to learn the way life moves,
And separation is evil, ruin, death.
So, since their life depends upon their union,
Their mutual bond, you must conclude their nature
Is also, in its very essence, joined.

Someone may tell you the body cannot feel,
Believing, so he says, that spirit mingled
All through the body is the only force
That knows sensation. All that's wrong with this
Is that it flies in the face of facts we know
Are obvious and true. Can anyone
Explain what bodily sensation is
Unless he trusts his own experience of it?
But with the spirit gone, body is left
Devoid of all sensation: it has lost
Something that was, in life, not all its own,
No more its own possession than other things
It loses with its death.

                        That eyes
Lack the ability to see a thing
And are really only outlooks for the spirit,
Is hard to say, and harder to believe,

Since their own feeling claims the opposite,
And their own feeling is the motive force
That pulls, or pushes, us to this point of view.
Sometimes, you know, we can't see dazzling objects
Through an excess of light; who ever heard
Of doorways, portals, outlooks, in such trouble?
Besides, if eyes are doorways, might it not
Be better to remove them, sash, jamb, lintel,
And let the spirit have a wider field?

Democritus, a sage heroic man,
Whose judgment we should honor and revere,
Told us one thing we never can accept,
Namely that motes of body and of spirit
Are placed in alternate sequence, one by one,
And in this way bind body and soul together.
Untrue: not only are the motes of spirit
Much smaller than those which form the body's substance,
But they are also fewer, here and there
At wider intervals throughout the framework.
To demonstrate how small and how close-knit
You might, indeed, go far enough to say
That the very least, the most diminutive
Bodies that rouse our sensitive response
Are much too gross, too large, to indicate
The closeness of the intervals wherein
The motes of spirit are held. We seldom feel
A single speck of dust, a grain of chalk
On thumb or finger-tip, the mist at night,
A spider's gossamer thread across our walk,
Bird's feathers, flying thistledown, all things
So light they make hard work of a descent.
We do not sense each footfall of the gnat,
Each loop of the measuring-worm across a forearm.
So it is true that there must be a stir
In many parts commingled through our bodies
Before the seeds of spirit are touched, can feel,
Can bounce across these intervals, clash, collide,

Rebound, unite, and once more leap apart.
Mind, rather than spirit, is more powerful,
More in control of life, for without mind,
Without intelligence, no part of spirit
Could dwell for even an instant in the limbs.
If mind departs, its loyal comrade, spirit,
Follows at once, vanishes into air,
And leaves the cold limbs in the chill of death,
But if a man has mind and intellect,
Though he may be a mutilated trunk,
A lopped and limbless torso, for all that
He is alive, he breathes the vital air.
The same holds true for a lacerated eye:
However badly slashed, it still can see
While the pupil stays intact; cut all around it,
You do no mortal harm, but once you damage
Its tiny central spot the light is gone,
Shadows obscure all residues of brightness.
In just this bond are mind and spirit joined.

You need to know that mind and spirit both
Are born in living creatures, and are mortal.
(I like this kind of teaching, though it takes time
To make my verses fully worthy of you.)
So, first of all, if I say *mind*, or *spirit*,
Consider them as one; they truly are,
Combined together, one mortal entity.
I have already shown how this is formed
Of the most tiny particles, smaller by far
Than those of water, mist, or smoke—much quicker,
More easily impelled, more apt to stir
From even fantasies of mist or smoke—
The kind of thing we look at in our dreams
When altars seem to lift a swirl of incense
(We are all, of course, the hosts of images.)

Now then: just as you see when jars are broken
Their wine or water flow in all directions,

As steam or smoke dissolve in the stir of air,
Believe that spirit also is diffused,
Is quick to perish, swift in dissolution
Into its primal elements, once it leaves
The limbs of man. The body, which we say
Is, as it were, its vase, can never hold it
Against exterior shock, can not withstand
Disintegration, once our veins are bloodless.
So how can you suppose an element
Like air, more unsubstantial than our bodies,
Could possibly have the power to hold the spirit?

We sense that body and mind are born together,
Together mature, together age. As children
Go purposeless, knock-kneed and wobbly creatures,
So their intelligence tags along; but grown
To sturdier years, their understanding broadens,
Their muscular and mental powers increase.
Later, when time's dominion shakes the body,
When limbs react with dull ungainliness,
Then the mind limps, tongue is a babbler, mind
Is palsied, all is failure, all is loss.
So spirit's quality must dissolve like smoke
Into the air aloft; as I have shown,
Its birth, its growth, its aging, and its death
Are one with ours.

              And in another way
Its life is like our own: as body suffers
Dreadful disease and racking pain, so mind
Knows grief, anxiety, horror, partnership
In death; when body is diseased, the mind
Often goes wandering a witless way,
Rages and rants, or in a torpor sinks
Deep into nodding drowsiness, wherein
It hears no voice, can recognize no face
Of those who stand around, and, through their tears,
Try to recall the dying soul to life.

Yes, mind indeed is mortal, and disease
Can enter it; disease and pain alike
Are, as we know, the artisans of death.
More tragi-comic is the case when wine
Takes hold of a man and burns his veins with fire.
His limbs grow heavy, his knees interfere
Each with the other, or buckle under him,
His tongue grows thick, his mind's a sot, his eyes
Go for a swim, he hiccups, slobbers, yells,
All this because the violence of wine
Has strength to stun the spirit in the body.
But things confused as easily as this,
As easily interfered with, clearly prove
That a rougher and more penetrative force
Might cause the shock of utter annihilation.
We have seen epileptics, whose disease
Is like a thunderbolt, which strikes them down.
The patient, in convulsions, foams at the mouth,
Groans, shudders, stiffens, twists, and gasps for breath,
Exhausts himself, jerks wildly in contortions
Because the terrible force of this disease,
Driven through all the limbs, expels the spirit
In the foam of the mouth, the way a great wind spews
Salt-froth from wave-crests. Deeper down, the limbs
Are on the rack of pain, and groans are heard
Under that torture; elements of speech,
Thickened or massed together, try to find
Their panic way out of the mouth, as words
And phrases do, in times more orderly.
Delirium occurs when mind and spirit
Are hopelessly confused, split, shattered, shocked
By that invading poison. After a while
The cause of the evil ebbs, the bitter taint
Returns to its old darkness, and the victim
Rises, still shaky, makes a little gain
From day to day, and finally is well.
Since a disease as great as this can strike,
Can toss the motes of spirit in the body,

Tear them apart in miserable ways,
And make them suffer, why do you believe
They can enjoy life in the empty air
Where the great winds go coursing? Mind, we see,
Like body, can be cured by medicine,
A fact which proves the life of mind is mortal.
Whoever tries to alter mind or soul,
Or seeks to bend any of nature's ways,
Must either add new parts, or change around
Their old arrangement, or take some away,
But things immortal never suffer change,
Nor can they, by their definition, vary.
If anything is changed, leaving its bounds,
That is the death of what it was before.
It makes no difference whether mind is sick
Or cured by medicine; as I have said,
Either condition proves its mortal nature.
The truth, it seems to me, not only meets
Falsehood head-on, but cuts off its retreat,
And so is doubly victor.

                    We often see
Men die by inches; toes and nails succumb
To lividness, next feet and legs, till soon
The other limbs feel the chill tread of death.
And since the same thing happens to the spirit,
Which never seems to issue, all at once,
Out of the body, it is also mortal.
Don't think it goes and hides itself, deep down
Within the limbs, withdraws its particles
All to one lair, leaving the body senseless.
If so, that place where so much spirit gathers
Ought to seem much more sensitive by far.
The truth is, no such area exists—
Spirit, if scattered to the air, expires.
(I have said this many, many times already)—
But even if I had a sort of notion
To grant a little armistice to falsehood

And let you say that spirit goes and hides
Deep down in bodies of the slowly dying,
You still will have to grant that spirit's mortal.
What difference does it make whether it dies
Dispersed through air, or shrinks, contracts, and dulls
Itself to nothing? Either way, its host,
Its human being, is left devoid of life.

Since mind, in fact, is part of man, one part,
Fixed in one definite place, like ears and eyes
And other senses regulating life—
Since hands, or eyes, or nostrils, have no feeling
Apart from us, and no existence either
Except a rapid wasting, so the mind
Cannot exist without a human body
To serve as urn, as vessel, for it. Make
A better metaphor, if you can, to serve you!

Together, body and mind, with quickened power,
Are joined, are strong, delight in life together.
Spirit can not engender viable motion
Without the body, nor, without the spirit,
Can body endure, or utilize the senses.
An eye, torn from the socket, can see nothing,
And neither, by themselves, can mind and spirit
Have any power. Their motes are held together
Through flesh and bone, through nerve and sinew; they
Cannot leap free: thus, being tension-fused,
They impart those drives, those movements of sensation
Which are impossible to them after death,
When they are loosed to air, for air is not
A body, cannot be, unless it holds
Spirit in such tight compass it can move
The way it did before, in flesh and sinews.
Sometimes, even within the body's bonds,
Spirit seems tired, or weakened for some reason,
And wants to get away; then faces pale,
Assume that last-hour look, and all the limbs

Collapse, in what we call a faint or swoon,
And all of us, in mortal terror, try
To keep the bonds of body and soul together.
At such a time the power of mind or spirit
Is frail as body, and a bit more pressure
Would bring it all to ruin. Well, then, why claim
That spirit, driven from the body, weak,
Unsheltered, can exist in emptiness
Not for all time, but even for a second?
Let me repeat—this you must face, own up to:
Without the body's armor, without the breath
Of life, both mind and spirit are bound to perish,
Sharing one common cause.

                          Nor can the body
Endure the loss of spirit, but decays
Into foul stinkingness; this should suffice
To prove that spirit seeps away like smoke
And while it goes the body changes, rots,
And its foundations crumble, even as spirit
Seeks its way out through every pore. Here's proof
That spirit scatters when it leaves the limbs,
Already broken in its bodily depths,
Before it makes its final way to air.
No dying man has ever felt his spirit
Rise, like a single lump, up to his chest,
His neck, his jaws; all he can sense is failure
Somewhere, in some fixed part; he also feels
His other senses lost in dissolution
Wherever they may be. But if our minds
Were of immortal stuff, they could not die,
Plaintive about their break-up, but would rather
Escape as from a prison, or slough off
Their old integument, like a snake renewed.

Next: why are mind and intellect and purpose
Never produced in heads or feet or hands,
But always, and in every man, are found

In the same fixed and definite areas?
There must be fixed locations for the birth
Of things, and fixed locations for their growth,
For their continuation; who wants legs
Emerging from his shoulders? Who wants fire
To spring from fountains or to father ice?

And furthermore: if spirit were immortal,
Sentient when separated from the body,
It would have to manage, somehow, with five senses.
Otherwise our imaginative powers
Could never visualize their wanderings
In Acheron below. Poets and painters,
For generations now, have shown these ghosts
With human attributes, but it seems to me
No bodiless unsubstantial phantom ever
Can possibly have eyes or hands or noses
Or tongues or self-sufficient listening ears.

Since therefore we feel sure that mind and soul
Pervade the entire body, that the whole
Is animated by their force, perhaps a blow
Is struck, so strong it cuts the body in two—
Undoubtedly, spirit is also halved,
Is shaken, split, from the bisected torso.
But something split, divided into parts,
Surely denies its nature is immortal.
It is said scythe-bearing battle-chariots,
Red-steaming from their killing course, can cut
Limbs off so quickly you can see them tremble
Or quiver on the ground, before their soldier
Has any inkling what has happened to him.
His fighting spirit pushes his attack
With what equipment he still has; he'll charge
And never know his left arm and his shield
Are swept off with marauding chariot-wheels
And scythes and horses, while, near by, a comrade
Lifts his right arm to scale a wall, and sees

His right arm isn't there, or attempts to rise
While his leg is kicking at him from the ground.
Even a severed head can lie in dust
With an alert expression, open-eyed,
Until the spirit is entirely lost.
You know how anger at a threatening snake
With darting tongue, long body, rattling tail,
Will make you take your sword, or knife, and hack it
To little bits, each one of which keeps writhing,
Staining the earth with venom, turning around
To strike itself, or heal the burn of its wound.
Are we going to say each of these little segments
Contains a complete spirit? That would seem
To make it follow that a single being
Has a whole host of spirits in his body.
Let's be more sensible: that which was split
At the same time as body, and divided
Into as many parts, we'd have to say
Was every bit as mortal as the body.

Besides, if spirit, by its very nature,
Possesses an immortal quality
Wherewith it slides from somewhere into our bodies
When we are being born, why can't we ever
Recall the time that went before, or keep
Any remembrance of those former ways?
But if the power of mind has changed so much
That all its memory of the past is gone,
It's wandering, I'd say, not far from death.
Give in, own up—that pre-existent spirit
Has perished, gone—and the spirit we have now
Is, we might say, a now (or new) creation.

A further point: if spirit's quickening power
Comes to us when gestation's term is finished,
When we are being born and crossing over
The threshold of the light, it seems unfit
For spirit to have seemed to grow with body,

Together with the limbs and in the blood
Through those dark months. Rather, it should have lived
In its own cavern, somewhere by itself,
While body was abundant with sensation!
How obviously and utterly false! The proof
Is manifest—through sinew, flesh, vein, bone,
Spirit is intertwined—why, even teeth
Are partners of its feeling; they can ache,
Hurt from cold water, bite too hard on shell
Or cherry-pit. I am almost tired of saying
Spirits are subject, like ourselves, to laws
Of birth and death. Their intimate connection
With body is too close for argument
That they were ever, so to speak, outsiders;
And being as close as this, it also follows
They never could go sauntering forth alone,
All by themselves, away from nerves, bones, joints.
Well, think so if you want to—that spirit comes
Sneaking from somewhere outside into us,
A percolation through our every limb!
Really, now? All the more then, I should think,
Having been fused with body it will die;
What percolates is dissolved, and therefore dies.
As food, dispersed through all the body's channels,
Distributed through the members, is absorbed,
Supplies a nature different from its own,
So mind and spirit, entering whole and new
Into a body, in their permeance
Become dissolved, dispersed through all those channels,
In particles by which the nature of spirit
Is generated, and, once born, is lord
Over our bodies, offspring of the mind
Which perished when distributed through our limbs.
Therefore, the spirit does not seem to lack
Its share of birthdays, and its share of death.

Are any seeds of spirit ever left
In a lifeless body? If there ever are,

They can't be called immortal, having lost
Part of themselves. But if the spirit goes,
Leaving no particle at all in body,
What makes worms issue from a rotting corpse?
Whence comes that boneless, bloodless horde, to bloat
The swollen limbs? Maybe you think that spirits
Sneak into worms from somewhere farther off,
Or you believe that, one by one, they troop
Into dead bodies, but you never wonder
Why spirits, by the tens of thousands, come
Where only one has left, though this would seem
To be a question well worth asking, one
Worth putting on the agenda: are the spirits
Hunters of worm-seed? Are they architects
Designing habitations there? Or squatters
Moving in on tenements already built?
No answer tells us why they act like this,
Going to all that trouble. Lacking body,
They fly about with no disease, no chill,
No hunger. It's the property of body
To suffer so, and mind shares many evils
From that contagion. Never mind, assume
Spirits make bodies for themselves to enter,
You still will have to tell us how they do it,
And there's no answer to that one. Therefore, spirits
Don't make themselves bodies and limbs, and do not
Creep into frames already formed, wherein
They'd find themselves, oh, most uncomfortable,
In quarters least commodious and convenient.

Why is the breed of lions violent,
Sullen or furious? Why are foxes sly,
Clever, astute? What makes the deer so swift,
So timorous? Why are all such traits and others
Consistent throughout all the generations?
It must be that in every stock and seed
The power of mind parallels growth of body,
But if mind were immortal, could exchange

One body for another, we would see
Some lovely freaks, a mastiff, scared to death,
Trying to flee a deer, or a fierce dove
Chasing a hawk, men would be asses, beasts
Perform like scholars. It is one big lie
To say immortal spirits change with body.
Change loosens things, makes them dissolve and die,
Parts are transposed, can move from their positions,
Submit to dissolution, and succumb.
Some men will tell you that the human souls
Transmigrate, always, into human bodies.
If so, I'd like to know why no damn fool
Ever becomes a sage, why schoolboys lack
Even common sense, or why no weanling colt
Has anything like a full-grown racer's power?
Well, one way out, of course, is to suggest
That mind goes soft if body is soft. If so,
You'll have to say that spirit must be mortal
Since, by its change among the body's limbs,
It loses much of its former life and feeling.
But how can the power of mind ever attain
The ripeness it desires, and grow with body
Unless they have been co-eval from the first?
Why should it want to escape from agèd limbs,
Why fear incarceration in a shell
Rotted by time, like a collapsing house?
But for immortal things there are no dangers.

It seems more than a trifle comical
To think that spirits come around in throngs
As stand-bys at the copulating rites
Or births of animals, and all agog
To be the first aboard; perhaps they have
Some mutual agreement, or each holds
A ticket for his place in line, to keep them
From scuffles, squabbles, and unseemly jostling!

Trees cannot root in sky, nor clouds exist
In deep sea-water, fish can't live in fields,

Nor blood in cords of wood, nor sap in rocks.
There is an everlasting fixed assignment,
A station set for being and growth. So mind
Can have no origin apart from body,
No independent nature, no existence
Out of the area of blood and sinew.
If, by some pre-arrangement, mind could choose
Its birthplace or its residence at will
In head or shoulders, or in toes or heels,
It still would be, and stay, in the same vessel,
The same container, Man. But since the rule
Seems to prevail, even within our bodies,
That there's a definite abiding-place
Where mind and spirit have to live and grow,
So much the less is it admissible
They can be brought to birth, or can endure
Outside the body. When the body dies,
Spirit, you must agree, is just as dead,
Just as disintegrate. How silly it is
To think that mortal and immortal can be joined
In everlasting covenant, can perform
In mutual partnership! What in all the world
Is more nonsensical, lunatic, insane
Than this idea that mortal and immortal
Unite in deathless and eternal pact
To bear up under the storms of devastation?
Is spirit kept immune from deadly things,
Never assailed by them? Do they retire
Driven back at their first onslaught, even before
Our sentinels challenge? Can this be the reason
We say that soul or spirit, is immortal?
Ah, we know better. Spirit often fails
With bodily diseases; even more,
Has troubles of its own, anxieties
About its future, fears, a sense of guilt
Over past sins, its own peculiar rage,
Its own forgetful spells, its own dark plunge
Into black waters of depression.

Death

Is nothing to us, has no relevance
To our condition, seeing that the mind
Is mortal. Just as, long ago, we felt
Not the least touch of trouble when the wars
Were raging all around the shaken earth
And from all sides the Carthaginian hordes
Poured forth to battle, and no man ever knew
Whose subject he would be in life or death,
Which doom, by land or sea, would strike him down,
So, when we cease to be, and body and soul,
Which joined to make us one, have gone their ways,
Their separate ways, nothing at all can shake
Our feelings, not if earth were mixed with sea
Or sea with sky. Perhaps the mind or spirit,
After its separation from our body,
Has some sensation; what is that to us?
Nothing at all, for what we knew of being,
Essence, identity, oneness, was derived
From body's union with spirit, so, if time,
After our death, should some day reunite
All of our present particles, bring them back
To where they now reside, give us once more
The light of life, this still would have no meaning
For us, with our self-recollection gone.
As we are now, we lack all memory
Of what we were before, suffer no wound
From those old days. Look back on all that space
Of time's immensity, consider well
What infinite combinations there have been
In matter's ways and groupings. How easy, then,
For human beings to believe we are
Compounded of the very selfsame motes,
Arranged exactly in the selfsame ways
As once we were, our long-ago, our now
Being identical. And yet we keep
No memory of that once-upon-a-time,
Nor can we call it back; somewhere between

A break occurred, and all our atoms went
Wandering here and there and far away
From our sensations. If there lies ahead
Tough luck for any man, he must be there,
Himself, to feel its evil, but since death
Removes this chance, and by injunction stops
All rioting of woes against our state,
We may be reassured that in our death
We have no cause for fear, we cannot be
Wretched in nonexistence. Death alone
Has immortality, and takes away
Our mortal life. It does not matter a bit
If we once lived before.

                        So, seeing a man
Feel sorry for himself, that after death
He'll be a rotting corpse, laid in a tomb,
Succumb to fire, or predatory beasts,
You'll know he's insincere, just making noise,
With rancor in his heart, though he believes,
Or tries to make us think so, that death ends all.
And yet, I'd guess, he contradicts himself,
He does not really see himself as gone,
As utter nothingness, but does his best—
Not really understanding what he's doing—
To have himself survive, for, in his life,
He will project a future, a dark day
When beast or bird will lacerate his corpse.
So he feels sorry for himself; he fails
To make the real distinction that exists
Between his castoff body, and the man
Who stands beside it grieving, and imputes
Some of his sentimental feelings to it.
Resenting mortal fate, he cannot see
That in true death he'll not survive himself
To stand there as a mourner, stunned by grief
That he is burned or mangled. If in death
It's certainly no pleasure to be mauled

By beak of bird or fang of beast, I'd guess
It's no voluptuous revel to be laid
Over the flames, or packed in honey and ice,
Stiff on the surface of a marble slab,
Or buried under a great mound of earth.

And men behave the same way at a banquet,
Holding the cups or garlanding the brows,
And sighing from the heart, "Ah, life is short
For puny little men, and when it goes
We cannot call it back," as if they thought
The main thing wrong, after their death, will be
That they are very thirsty, or may have
A passionate appetite for who knows what.
"No longer will you happily come home
To a devoted wife, or children dear
Running for your first kisses, while your heart
Is filled with sweet unspoken gratitude.
You will no longer dwell in happy state,
Their sword and shield. Poor wretch," men tell themselves,
"One fatal day has stolen all your gains."
But they don't add, "And all your covetings."
If they could see this clearly, follow it
With proper reasoning, their minds would be
Free of great agony and fear, "As now
You lie asleep in death, forevermore
You will be quit of any sickening pain,
While we, who stood beside your funeral pyre,
Have, with no consolation, mourned your death
In sorrow time will never heal." Well, then,
Ask of your dead what bitterness he finds
In sleep and quiet; why should anyone
Wear himself out in everlasting grief?
No man, when body and soul are lost in sleep,
Finds himself missing, or conducts a search
For his identity; for all we know,
For all we care, that sleep might last forever
And we would never list ourselves as missing.

Yet, all this while, our motes, our atoms, wander
Not far from sense-producing shift and stir,
And suddenly we come to wakefulness.
So we must think of death as being nothing,
As less than sleep, or less than nothing, even,
Since our array of matter never stirs
To reassemble, once the chill of death
Has taken over.

       Hark! The voice of Nature
Is scolding us: "What ails you, little man,
Why this excess of self-indulgent grief,
This sickliness? Why weep and groan at death?
If you have any sense of gratitude
For a good life, if you can't claim her gifts
Were dealt you in some kind of riddled jar
So full of cracks and holes they leaked away
Before you touched them, why not take your leave
As men go from a banquet, fed to the full
On life's good feast, come home, and lie at ease,
Free from anxiety? Alas, poor fool,
If, on the other hand, all of your joys
Are gone, and life is only wretchedness,
Why try to add more to it? Why not make
A decent end? There's nothing, it would seem,
My powers can contrive for your delight.
The same old story, always. If the years
Don't wear your body, don't corrode your limbs
With lassitude, if you keep living on
For centuries, if you never die at all,
What's in it for you but the same old story
Always, and always?" How could we reply
To this, except to say that Nature's case
Is argued to perfection? Now suppose
Some older man, a senior citizen,
Were plaintiff, wretcheder than he ought to be,
Lamenting death, would Nature not be right
To cry him down, with even sharper voice,

"Why, you old scoundrel, take those tears of yours
Somewhere away from here, cut out the whining.
You have had everything from life, and now
You find you're going to pieces. You desire,
Always, what isn't there; what is, you scorn,
So life has slipped away from you, incomplete,
Unsatisfactory, and here comes death,
An unexpected summoner, to stand
Beside you, long before you want to leave,
Long, long, before you think you've had enough.
Let it all go, act as becomes your age,
Be a great man, composed; give in; you must."
Such a rebuke from Nature would be right,
For the old order yields before the new,
All things require refashioning from others.
No man goes down to Hell's black pit; we need
Matter for generations yet to come,
Who, in their turn, will follow you, as men
Have died before you and will die hereafter.
So one thing never ceases to arise
Out of another; life's a gift to no man
Only a loan to him. Look back at time—
How meaningless, how unreal!—before our birth.
In this way Nature holds before our eyes
The mirror of our future after death.
Is this so grim, so gloomy? Is it not
A rest more free from care than any sleep?

Now all those things which people say exist
In Hell, are really present in our lives.
The story says that Tantalus, the wretch,
Frozen in terror, fears the massive rock
Balanced in air above him. It's not true.
What happens is that in our lives the fear,
The silly, vain, ridiculous fear of gods,
Causes our panic dread of accident.
No vultures feed on Tityos, who lies

Sprawled out for them in Hell; they could not find
In infinite eternities of time
What they are searching for in that great bulk,
Nine acres wide, or ninety, or the spread
Of all the globe. No man can ever bear
Eternal pain, nor can his body give
Food to the birds forever. We do have
A Tityos in ourselves, and lie, in love,
Torn and consumed by our anxieties,
Our fickle passions. Sisyphus, too, is here
In our own lives; we see him as the man
Bent upon power and office, who comes back
Gloomy and beaten after every vote.
To seek for power, such an empty thing,
And never gain it, suffering all the while,
This is to shove uphill the stubborn rock
Which over and over comes bouncing down again
To the flat levels where it started from.
Or take another instance: when we feed
A mind whose nature seems unsatisfied,
Never content, with all the blessings given
Through season after season, with all the charms
And graces of life's harvest, this, I'd say,
Is to be like those young and lovely girls,
The Danaids, trying in vain to fill
Their leaky jars with water. Cerberus,
The Furies, and the dark, and the grim jaws
Of Tartarus, belching blasts of heat—all these
Do not exist at all, and never could.
But here on earth we do fear punishment
For wickedness, and in proportion dread
Our dreadful deeds, imagining all too well
Being cast down from the Tarpeian Rock,
Jail, flogging, hangmen, brands, the rack, the knout;
And even though these never touch us, still
The guilty mind is its own torturer
With lash and rowel, can see no end at all

To suffering and punishment, and fears
These will be more than doubled after death.
Hell does exist on earth—in the life of fools.

You well might think of saying to yourself:
"Even good Ancus closed his eyes on the light—
A better man than you will ever be,
You reprobate—and many lords and kings
Rulers of mighty nations, all have died.
Even that monarch, who once paved the way
Making the sea a highway for his legions
Where foot and horse alike could march dry-shod
While the deep foamed and thundered at the outrage,
Even he, great Xerxes, died and left the light,
And Scipio, the thunderbolt of war,
Terror of Carthage, gave his bones to earth
As does the meanest lackey. Add to these
Philosophers and artists, all the throng
Blessed by the Muses; Homer's majesty
Lies low in the same sleep as all the rest.
Democritus, warned by a ripe old age
That, with his memory, his powers of mind
Were also failing, gave himself to death;
And Epicurus perished, that great man
Whose genius towered over all the rest,
Making their starry talents fade and die
In his great sunlight. Who are you, forsooth,
To hesitate, resent, protest your death?
Your life is death already, though you live
And though you see, except that half your time
You waste in sleep, and the other half you snore
With eyes wide open, forever seeing dreams,
Forever in panic, forever lacking wit
To find out what the trouble is, depressed,
Or drunk, or drifting aimlessly around."

Men seem to feel some burden on their souls,
Some heavy weariness; could they but know

Its origin, its cause, they'd never live
The way we see most of them do, each one
Ignorant of what he wants, except a change,
Some other place to lay his burden down.
One leaves his house to take a stroll outdoors
Because the household's such a deadly bore,
And then comes back, in six or seven minutes—
The street is every bit as bad. Now what?
He has his horses hitched up for him, drives,
Like a man going to a fire, full-speed,
Off to his country-place, and when he gets there
Is scarcely on the driveway, when he yawns,
Falls heavily asleep, oblivious
To everything, or promptly turns around,
Whips back to town again. So each man flees
Himself, or tries to, but of course that pest
Clings to him all the more ungraciously.
He hates himself because he does not know
The reason for his sickness; if he did,
He would leave all this foolishness behind,
Devote his study to the way things are,
The problem being his lot, not for an hour,
But for all time, the state in which all men
Must dwell forever and ever after death.

Finally, what's this wanton lust for life
To make us tremble in dangers and in doubt?
All men must die, and no man can escape.
We turn and turn in the same atmosphere
In which no new delight is ever shaped
To grace our living; what we do not have
Seems better than everything else in all the world,
But should we get it, we want something else.
Our gaping thirst for life is never quenched.
We have to know what luck next year will bring,
What accident, what end. But life, prolonged,
Subtracts not even one second from the term
Of death's continuance. We lack the strength

To abbreviate that eternity. Suppose
You could contrive to live for centuries,
As many as you will. Death, even so,
Will still be waiting for you; he who died
Early this morning has as many years
Interminably before him, as the man,
His predecessor, has, who perished months
Or years, or even centuries ago.

Book IV

Exploring ways where none have gone before,
Across the Muses' realms I make my way,
Happy to come to virgin springs, to drink
Their freshness, to discover all the flowers
No man has ever seen, and of them twine
Myself a garland, which no poet yet
Has had from any Muse. This I deserve
Because I teach great things, because I strive
To free the spirit, give the mind release
From the constrictions of religious fear,
Because I write clear verse about dark things,
Enduing what I touch with grace and charm;
And this makes sense, for, just as doctors do,
When they give bitter wormwood to a child,
But first take pains to smear the rim of the cup
With the sweet golden honey, and to fool
The unsuspecting patient, anyway
As far as the lips, till he gulps down the dose
Of bitter wormwood, fooled, but not betrayed,
But rather given health and strength, so I,
Harsh as my system may appear to those
Who have not used it (and, in general,
People shrink back, set lips and minds against it)
Nevertheless, for your sake, Memmius,
Have wanted to explain the way things are
Turning the taste of honey into sound
As musical, as golden, so that I
May hold your mind with poetry, while you
Are learning all about that form, that pattern,
And see its usefulness.

Since I have taught
What the mind's nature is, and from what source
Its strength derives, united with the body,
And how, when severed from the body, it reverts
To primal elements, I now begin
To teach you about images, so-called,
A subject of most relevant importance.
These images are like a skin, or film,
Peeled from the body's surface, and they fly
This way and that across the air; they cause
A terror in our minds, whether we wake
Or in our sleep see fearful presences.
The replicas of those who have left the light
Haunt us and startle us horribly in dreams.
But let us never think, by any chance,
That souls escape from Acheron, or shades
Flutter and flit around with living men.
Let us have no delusions of a life
After our death, when body and mind have gone
Their separate ways, each to its primal source.

Let me repeat: these images of things,
These almost airy semblances, are drawn
From surfaces; you might call them film, or bark,
Something like skin, that keeps the look, the shape
Of what it held before its wandering.
This should be obvious to the dullest mind
Since many things, as our own eyes can see,
Throw off a substance, rather coarse at times—
As burning wood produces smoke or steam—
And sometimes thinner, more condensed, the way
Cicadas cast their brittle summer jackets
Or calves at birth throw off the caul, or snakes
Slide out and leave their vesture under the brambles
Where we have often seen them, crumpled or caught.
This being so, some film of likeness, frail
And thin, must be sent forth from every surface.
It would make no sense for things as heavy as bark

Or even snakeskin to be shed, and found
Far from their origin, while other things
Are so minute, so very many in number,
So superficial, and can fly so fast
There seems to be no change in the arrangement
Of that from which they came; they keep that shape
And move with greater speed, being less hindered
Because they are so few, so near the surface.
And there are other things we see thrown out,
Not only from some depth, as we have said,
But also from an outermost surface—color,
To take one instance: watch the yellow awnings,
The reds, the purples, spread on poles and beams
In some great theatre, where they flutter, billow,
Stir, over the audience, and stain and dye
Not only actors, but with wavering hues
Transform the most distinguished senators
Watching the show; and where the walls are hung
Most thick with color, so much more the day
Indoors appears to smile in all that light
Of lovely radiance. If such hues as these
Are cast from curtain draperies, it must follow
All things project such likeness of themselves,
However unsubstantial, from their surface.
So there are, all around us, shapes and forms
Of definite outline, always on the move,
Delicate, small, woven of thread so rare
Our sight cannot detect them.
Other projections, odor, heat, and smoke,
And all things like them, swirl in shapeless clouds
Because their origin is deeper down,
With greater obstacles to fight against
And no wide sweep of highway for their concourse.
But when a veil, a delicate film of color,
Casts itself loose, there is no interference
To rip or tear it; easily it moves
From the advantage of its outerness.
And, finally, those replicas we see

In mirrors, water, and the brightnesses
Of any shining substance—all must be
Projections of originals, possessed
Of the same outer semblances. So there are
Most delicate forms, their semblances, whose motes,
Whose particles, invisible to all,
Still, in their sum, their total of recoil,
Dense and continual, convey to us
A vision, as from the surface of a mirror,
And this must surely be the only way
For duplication of such likenesses.

Now learn how very frail an image is,
How delicate in its nature. First of all,
Since atoms are beneath our power of sight,
So infinitely smaller than our eyes
Can ever begin to have the slightest glimpse of,
Let me extend the argument. I'll try
To be as brief as possible, but listen.
How small can anything be? We know of creatures
So tiny they would seem to disappear
If they were less than half their present size.
How big do you suppose their livers are?
Their hearts? The pupils of their eyes? Their toes?
Pretty minute, you must admit. Well, then,
What about things like those atomic motes
That form the elements of mind and spirit?
Diminutive, to say the least. Nor can we
Find with our finger tips the cause of smell
That clings there from the touch of marigold,
Centaury, heal-all, wormwood, southernwood.
So images move beyond our powers of sight.

They are not the only wanderers, these casts
From substance like themselves; there are other things,
Self-generated, in our atmosphere,
Forming themselves in many ways, aloft,

Changing incessantly, fluent, volatile,
Such as the cumulation of the clouds
Massing on high and darkening the earth
While gentling air with motion. You might say
Sometimes they look like shadows of the Giants
Scowling in flight, or mountains on parade
Before the sun, or monsters hauling rainstorms.

But I digress. Let us return again
To images, their quickness and their ease,
Their everlasting glide and flow, their smooth
Streaming from every surface. There is nothing
That does not set them stirring, and they move
Sometimes most easily through other things,
Glass, for example; but on rock or wood
They are shattered, broken, lost. But if they find
A shining solid object in their way,
A mirror, for example, they react
In different fashion, neither passing through
As glass would let them pass, nor broken up
By obdurate wood or rock, but, safe and sound
By virtue of the brightness, bounding back
Once more in our direction. Be as quick
As ever you can, confront your looking glass
With any object, there it is, at once
Reflected, all the tiny likenesses
In constancy of infinitesimal weave
Ebbing forever from their surfaces.
So many images in such little room!
Such swiftness in their origin! The sun
Is like them in the way he floods the world
With never an intermission in the rain
Of light-fall; so, from many other things,
The instantaneous reflections move
In all directions, bright and wonderful.
No matter where the mirror turns, we find
Response from similar form and hue.

                                    Besides,
After the clearest weather, when a storm
Pollutes the nasty air, and makes you think
All hell has puked its blackness up to fill
The bowls and craters of the sky, so foul,
So dark the night, so fearful, who can say
How much is cloud, how much of it cloud's image?
We can't make sense of this.

                            Some other problems:
How swiftly is an image borne along?
What speed is given its flight across the air?
How long a space, how brief a time, is used
As each with different aim pursues its course?
In answering, I'll try to have my verse
Be sweetly-spoken, but not long; I'll take
Swans for my model, not the honking cranes
Raucous in flight among the southern clouds.
Frail objects, formed from tiny particles,
Move swiftly: for example, light and heat
Are in this category, and their motes
Keep being shoved along through air by others,
Light after light, and flash pursuing flash,
In comet-like processional. Like these,
The images must cross tremendous space
In time almost dimensionless. This happens
Because they need only the slightest push,
The least ungentle impulse from behind
To set them going; once they're on their way
They are so rare of texture, so refined,
They meet no opposition anywhere,
They are all-pervasive in air's intervals.
Even those motes which come from deeper down
Within their sources, such as light and heat,
All seem to move, in a split-second's time,
In flight across the land and sea, in flood
Across the sky; how much more swiftly, then,
Goes the procession of the images,

All ready at their surfaces, prepared
With nothing to delay their taking-off,
No struggle, no long run before they rise,
As light as birds, into all kinds of space
In the same time that sunlight floods the sky.
Ah, look about you! Watch a glimmering pool
In the first shine of starlight, see the stars
Respond that very instant, radiant
In water's universe. Does this not prove
How marvelous the swift descent from heaven?
Our other senses know of emanance
In fragrances, in sunlight's heat, in surge
Of surf destroying sea-walls, in the sound
Of voices calling always through the air,
In salt-spray tasted as we walk the shore,
In bitterness imagined, when our eyes
Watch someone pouring wormwood into water,
So from all things there is this constant flow,
This all-pervasive issue, no delay,
No interruption, and our sense responds
In recognition.

       In the dark a form,
Something we touch or handle, seems to be
The same as what we look at in the light
Of full bright day; accordingly, we must
Infer a similar cause for sight and touch.
Suppose, in the dark, we touch a square, and find
Our sense responsive to it; given light,
Confronted by a square, what would we see
Except its image? For the cause of sight
Inheres in images; nothing can be seen
Without them; they are carried everywhere,
They go in all directions. But because
We apprehend them only with our eyes,
Wherever we look, all objects strike our gaze
With shape and color. Furthermore, we learn
From images what distance is, how far

One thing is from another or ourselves.
The way it works is this: the image drives
The air that lies before it through our eyes,
Brushing our pupils as it passes through,
And so we see how far away things are—
The greater the amount of air, the longer
The brushing process occupies, why, then,
The farther off the object of our sight
Will have to be. Oh, beyond any doubt
This happens with a most surprising speed
So that we recognize in the same moment
The kind of object and its distance from us.
We cannot see each detail, yet the sum
Is clear enough, and this is not so strange
If we remember how the wind and cold
Assail us, and we feel, not every twinge,
Not every single stab, but as it were
A constant pressure, as if an outside force
Were swarming all about us. If we stub
A toe against a stone, the thing we touch
Is, actually, only the outer shell,
The surface hue—but that's not what we feel—
Nothing that superficial—but instead
The inner hardness central to the rock.

Why does the image seem beyond the glass
As certainly it does? This corresponds
To the way things are visible through doors
When they are open, and we have a view
Of much that is outside. This view appears
Through twin or double air, which first we see
On our side of the doorposts, then of course
We see the doorposts, right and left, and next
The light beyond will brush our eyes, the air
Be different, and at last we catch a glimpse
Of the real things outdoors. In just this way
The image of the glass projects itself
Until it strikes our eyes, and, as it comes,

Pushes before it all the air between.
All this we see before we see the mirror,
But once we sense the glass, an image flies
Backward to it from us, rebounds, once more
Pushing the air before it, so we have
This sense of depth, of space beyond the glass.
All very simple, if we keep in mind ╲
The concept of the double flow of air.

What about right and left? How does it happen
Your right arm lifts, in a kind of pass,
And a southpaw waves at you out of the glass?
Let's see. An image, when it strikes the mirror
Is not completely turned around, the way
That you or I, confronted by a wall,
Would turn, but, rather, is pushed directly back,
Turned inside out by the pressure, as the nose
Or chin of a false-face would reverse itself
And point the other way, if gale-force wind
Or some explosion blew its features in.
You know, like an umbrella. There are times
When images may, in succession, move
From one glass to another, three, four, five,
Six times or more—most useful in a search
Since things, however hidden, cached away
In the recesses of a house, are found,
If you have mirrors enough, and brought to light
Around all turns and winding passages.
Also, by doubling mirrors, you can get
Your lefts and rights the way they really are,
And certain glasses, rounded like our sides,
Return a proper image, left for left
And right for right. I'm not entirely sure
Just why this happens—maybe, in some way,
They are really double, or perhaps their smooth
Sleek roundedness will let an image turn
With greater ease and in its natural way.
As for the fact that images, it seems,

Keep step with us, or imitate our gestures,
Why not? It's most unlikely they'd return
To some place we've just left; they cannot do it,
Nature compels them always to respond
Directly, from their coign of incidence.

The eyes avoid bright objects, try to shield
Themselves against them. If you stare too long
The sun will blind you by its mighty power—
And also since its images are borne
With violent downward impetus—to strike
And discompose the structure of the eyes.
Any sharp brightness often stings the eyes
Because it holds the seeds of fire, which pain
By penetration. Jaundiced people see
Everything tinged a bilious yellow color
Because their eyes emit a constant stream
Of particles thus hued which clash and fuse
With images they meet, confounding sense
And painting all things with their sallowness.
How is it we can stand in dark and see
Bright things beyond? Because the murkiness,
Being closer to us, fills our open eyes
To start with, but the bright and shining air
Follows in less than seconds, and this clears
Our vision, washes all the dark away,
For light is much more mobile, is composed
Of finer particles, yet has more power,
And once it clears the roadways of the eyes,
Removing the dark barriers and blocks,
At once the images of things begin
To move in our direction, driving on
Out of the light to help us see. From light
We can't see into darkness, for that air
Is slower-moving, thicker, bound to fill
All openings, so no images can move
Across the solid massiveness of dark.
Another thing: sometimes we see, far off,

The towers of a city, and our gaze
Makes them look rounded, though of course we know
They are foursquare and angular. But space
Tends to blunt angles, dull the images
In their long rushing toward us, wear them down,
Or maybe even never let us see them,
Rubbing them out by the continual sweep
Of air against them, so an angle seems
An arc, and masonry looks columnar—
Not with true roundness like things close at hand,
But vague and shadowy. This might suggest
How our own shadow seems to us to move
In sunlight following our course, our gesture—
If you believe that air, deprived of light,
Can move in such a way; what we call shadow
Is lightless air and nothing else. The ground,
In certain places, finds the sun blocked off
While we walk by, and fills with light again
As we move on, and so our shadow seems
To follow at our heels; new rays of light
Are always pouring out and vanishing
As quick as fluff in candle flame. The ground,
Easily robbed of light, as easily
Is filled again as the black shades dissolve.

We don't admit the eyes are fallible,
Not even an iota, in this case.
Their only function is to recognize
Where light and shadow are; they have no power
To recognize the way things really are,
To judge if light remains the same, or shade
Succeeds a predecessor: that, I've said,
Is something reason has to figure out.
So don't blame flaws of judgment on your eyes.
The ship we sail on does not seem to move,
The anchored one we pass seems flying by,
And with our sails or oars we make the hills,
The beaches, fly astern. Look at the stars—

All of them steadfast in the vaulted air,
Or so it seems—and yet we know they move
From rising to descent, far off, far down,
After their bright parade across the sky,
And sun and moon to our illusion seem
Halted, unmoving, not the wayfarers
Which our experience knows they really are.
And mountains, far across a reach of sea,
Look like one island, though we know that fleets
Could sail the roads between them. Children, dizzy
After they stop spinning themselves around,
Think that the rooms revolve, the pillars whirl,
And even ceilings threaten to fall down.
When nature starts to raise that ruddy disk
With wavering fires across the mountain-tops,
Those very summits which the sun appears
To touch, no farther off from where we stand
Than twice a thousand bowshots, or perhaps
Even less than that, make it five hundred times
As far as record-holders toss a javelin,
Hold in those areas below that sun
Infinite plains of air, unbounded shores,
Continents, populations, wilderness.
But a little puddle, half a knuckle deep,
Between a couple of cobbles after rain,
Reflects a panorama that appears
To go deep underground, descending down
As far as heaven is high, with clouds and sun
And marvellous strange subterranean stars.
Suppose your horse stops in a rushing stream
Halfway across, and you look down to see
The current sweeping past you, it appears
You still are riding on against the flow;
The run of the water and all things ashore
On either bank are keeping pace beside you.
Or take the pillars of a portico,
All the same height, all the same width apart,

And yet they seem with distance to contract,
Diminish, come together, roof to floor
And right to left, till the last thing you see
Is no more than a cone's tip. Mariners
At watch on voyage see the sun both rise
And set in water. Well, why not? Don't think
Their senses must be wrecked or derelict—
What else is there to see but sky and ocean?
And harbor folk, who do not know the sea,
But look at vessels riding at their moorings
Think they are all disabled underneath
The waterline, though oars and rudders seem
Like all the superstructure straight and firm,
While everything below is bent, concave,
Distorted by refraction. When the winds
Sweep scattered clouds across the sky at night,
The stars appear to swim against that drift,
Gliding above them, almost opposite
To their true course. The pressure of a hand
Beneath an eye makes everything you see
Come double to your gaze: the lighted lamps,
The chairs, the tables; guests and servants seem
To have, each one, two heads apiece, two bodies.
And, finally, in sleep, when all our limbs
Lie utterly relaxed, in dreams we find
Ourselves awake, moving about, aware
Of sun and daylight in the darkest murk,
Exchange our narrow mattress for the sky,
Sea, rivers, mountains, hike across the fields,
Hear sounds in night's relentless silences,
Converse while saying nothing. Oh, there are
Many examples of illusion's craft
Whereby we are beguiled to doubt our senses.
A vain endeavor, really; on the whole,
We are fooled, or fool ourselves, because we bring
Such predilections with us that we see
Imagined things, not real ones. Humankind

Finds nothing harder than to separate
The patent facts from those dubieties
Mind loves to introduce.

                    But if a man
Argues that, therefore, nothing can be known,
He does not really even know that much
Since he's confessing total ignorance.
I'd best not argue with this kind of man
Who sticks his head in the ground, his feet in the air.
Still, let me grant he knows this much, I'll ask
How, since he's never caught one glimpse of truth
In anything whatever, how does he know
What knowing and non-knowing are, what fact
Gave him the notion of the true and false,
Assured him of a difference between
The doubtful and the certain? You will find
All knowledge of the truth originates
Out of the senses, and the senses are
Quite irrefutable. Find, if you can,
A standard more acceptable than sense
To sort out truth from falsehood. What can be
More credible than sense? Shall reasoning,
Born of some error, some delusionment,
Argue the senses down? Ridiculous!
If sense is false, reason will have to be.
Can ears refute the eyes, the sense of touch
Negate the sense of hearing? Do our noses
Appeal against our eyes, our sense of taste
File counterclaim against our ears' report?
I'd hardly think so. To each sense belongs
Its jurisdiction, so that soft, hot, cold,
Color, sound, shape, and odor are assigned
To different areas. Therefore, no sense
Can contradict another or itself,
Since their report must be dependable
The same way always. If at any time
A thing seems true to them, it must be so.

And if your reasoning faculties can find
No explanation why a thing looks square
When seen close up, and round when farther off,
Even so, it might be better for a man
Who lacks the power of reason, to give out
Some idiotic theory, than to drop
All hold of basic principles, break down
Every foundation, tear apart the frame
That holds our lives, our welfare. All is lost,
Not only reason, but our very life,
Unless we have the courage and the nerve
To trust the senses, to avoid those sheer
Downfalls into the pits and tarns of nonsense.
All that verbose harangue against the senses
Is utter absolute nothing.

                If a building
Were planned by someone with a crooked ruler
Or an inaccurate square, or spirit-level
A little out of true, the edifice,
In consequence, would be a frightful mess,
Warped, wobbly, wish-wash, weak and wavering,
Waiting a welter of complete collapse—
So let your rule of reason never be
Distorted by the fallacies of sense
Lest all your logic prove a road to ruin.

As for the other senses, it's no task
To demonstrate how each enacts its part.
Take sound, to start with. Noise is audible
Because its body penetrates the ears,
Impinging on the sense; voices and sounds
Are bodily in nature, since they strike
With impact on the senses. Furthermore,
A cry can scrape the throat, or a harsh voice
Abrade the windpipe, as the sound proceeds
Out of the body. This is natural
Because the primal particles of voice,

As speech is formed, are massed in such array,
Such overplus, they jam the portals, rasp
Against the frames of egress. Words and tones,
Since they can hurt, are, beyond any doubt,
Made of material stuff. You know, of course,
How a man suffers loss of weight and strength
If he keeps roaring all the livelong day
From dawn-glow to the shadow of black night.
Voice, therefore, must be bodily, since loss
Of body follows from its overuse.
Rough voices have rough motes, and smoother ones
Have smoother elements. The ear is struck
By different sorts of atoms when a horn
Is muted, crooning low, or blares away
Full blast, or when the swans in plaintive cry
Raise their clear dirges over Helicon.
So, when our utterance sends voices forth
From deep within our bodies, turns them loose
Directly through our opened mouths, the tongue,
That quick and deft artificer of words,
Makes them articulate, and his designs
Are aided by the lips. When voices move
Not too far from their point of origin,
Each syllable is clearly heard, each sound
Easily recognized, each vocal shape
Keeps its identity; but if the space
Extends too far and words must find their way
Through multitudinous air, they blur to noise,
To sound still audible but meaningless.
Another thing: one word, one crier's call
Will often stir the ears of many men
In a large audience; one voice become
Multiplied into many through the ears
Of many listeners; yet now and then
Phrases or words escape or murmurs die,
Or sounds confronted by some barrier
Are beaten back, rebound almost, like words
In some loud foreign language no one knows.

Once you have witnessed this phenomenon
You can explain how in some lonely place
The rocks repeat our voices word for word,
When we are calling for our comrades, lost,
Scattered, astray in mountain darknesses,
While we keep shouting. I have sometimes heard
As many as six or seven echoes cry
In answer to one voice. So hills to hills
Redound and bounce reiteration back
Each to the other till the nearby folk
Invent the presences of goatfoot gods,
Satyrs and nymphs and fauns, night-wandering,
Whose rumpuses and rowdy pranks, they swear
To the last man, disturb the peace at night;
And they go on to talk about the sound
Of music, sweet and sad, the twang of strings
The pipes, the singing voices. Far away,
If you believe their stories, farmer-folk
Listen while Pan, nodding his shaggy head
With the pine needles hanging over his ears,
Keeps time, lips up and down the open reeds
So that the woodland melodies pour out
With never a silence. No man likes to think
His home is some forgotten wilderness
Abandoned even by gods, and this is why
They toss around these marvels in their talk,
These stories of the weird and wonderful.
Or it may be some other reason works
To lead them on, for all the human race
Is overeager in its greed to fill
The listening ear.

                But let's go on to say
There's nothing wonderful about the fact
That voices pass through spaces where the eyes
Can see no object plain. Behind closed doors
Talk is perceptible, because the voice
Can fare intact along those winding ways

Where images would balk, or shatter themselves,
As happens when they are given no straight aisles,
No sheets of glass to swim through. And one voice
Divides itself or multiplies (no matter)
In all directions, many born of one,
The way a spark can kindle many fires.
So places where no sight intrudes may teem
With resonant voices. Images must move,
Once they are set in motion, straight ahead,
So nobody can see beyond a wall
Though he can hear the words pass through, but these,
Even so, all run together, dull and blurred,
Blunt inarticulate sounds, not truly words.

It is every bit as easy to explain
Our sense of taste; the palate and the tongue
Supply the apparatus. In our mouths
We crush the flavor from the food we chew,
Something like squeezing water from a sponge,
So that the product, all of it, seeps through
The palate's pores, the tongue's interstices.
If this diffused material is made
Out of smooth particles, we find it sweet
Around the tongue, but if the motes are rough,
We have the sense of acid, sour and sharp.
This pain or pleasure never goes beyond
The limits of the palate. Down the throat
Is out of mind; the subsequent procedure
Offers no gourmet exquisite delights.
It makes no difference at all what food,
Soggy or crisp, tasteless or seasoned well,
Gives nutriment to the body; all that counts
Is whether it's digestible, and keeps
The gastric juices flowing.

                              One man's meat,
The proverb says, only too often proves
Another's poison. Different creatures find

The same food sweet or sour, delicious, nasty.
I've heard about a curious kind of snake
That you can kill simply by spitting on it,
Which makes it bite itself to suicide;
And quails and goats wax fat on hellebore,
To man a deadly poison. Don't forget
What I have said before, but bear in mind
That all the first beginnings of all things
Are held and mixed in many different ways,
And as all food-consuming animals
Differ in looks, in contour, size and shape,
According to their breed, we must suppose
Their basic elements are different,
Not only from our own, but also even
Among themselves, with wider intervals
Or narrower ones, in all their limbs, as well
As in their tongues and palates. Some are large
And some are small, and some triangular;
And some are square, and some are round, and some
Irregular polygons; for as their scheme
Of shape and movement indicates, they must
Adapt themselves to different passageways,
Proceed by channels varying with their forms,
So, when to some a food is sweet, but others
Make faces at its bitterness, the cause
Must be that in the former case the motes
Are very smooth, enter the palate's pores
Most tractably, most gently gliding by,
While those who find the same thing in their mouths
Harsh and distasteful must have felt the barbs,
Hooks, jags of roughness as they gulped them down.
Apply this general principle—you'll find
The problems easy. If a fever mounts
From an excess of bile, or a disease
Is stirred up in some other way, the body
Becomes a hotbed of confusion, all
Its basic elements seem to insist
On changing their positions; those that once

Produced a pleasant sense reaction now
Lose force; and others, penetrating, cause
The different response of bitterness.
Honey is an example; it contains
Both elements, a sweet and bitter blend,
(As I have told you—all too many times.)

As for the sense of smell, there must be, first,
More than one source from which all odors flow
Like rivers, or are sprinkled like the rain.
And odors differ in the ways they please
Different creatures, for their varied forms
Are different, so bees, from far away,
Swarm to the scent of honey, but the reek
Of carrion draws buzzards. The split hoof
Of deer or boar will set the coursing hounds
Nosing along the trail; and the white goose,
Once saviour of our Roman citadel,
Detects far off the scent of human beings.
Thus different creatures, led by different scents,
Are led to their own food, or are warned off
From ugly poisons. So the races of wild beasts
Are kept alive.

              Of all the smells there are
Some carry farther than others, but not one
Reaches as far as voice or sound or sight
(That last, I think, I hardly need to mention).
For odors come on wandering courses, slow
In their approach, are easily dispersed,
Fade in the air; one reason is, they start
From inner depths, and even seem to have
Some trouble in emerging; possibly
They even tend back to their source again.
We know that stronger odors emanate
From things when crushed, or ground, or burnt in fire,
And odors must be made of larger motes
Than voices, since they do not pass through stone

Where sound can penetrate, and it's not easy,
At times, to find the whereabouts of a smell
Since odors are no hot-foot messengers,
But dawdlers, and their trails grow cold in air,
Too vague, too wavering for the nosing hounds
Unless they pause and check and cast about.

I should have pointed out, a short while back,
That taste and smell are not the only senses
Which vary or conflict in their effect,
Please some and rankle in others. It's the same
With light and color. Lions, for example,
Those wild and ravening creatures, cannot bear
To see a rooster, watch him flap his wings,
Sound his bright clarion summons to the dawn.
They'll panic at the sight, they'll run away
Dusting the veldt with terror. Roosters cast,
(At least the lions think so) little darts
Or quills from every atom of their bodies
And these get in a lion's eyes, and sting,
And smart and burn so much—the hardiest beast
Cannot endure the agony. But men
Have no such trouble; no such particles
Can hurt us in the least; our irises
May be too strong for them to penetrate
Or if they do they come right out again
Too soon for any irritating stay.

Next, learn (this can be brief) what moves the mind,
How things that come there do so. Let me say
To start with that the images of things
Are, many of them, vagrant, and they move
In all directions and in many ways
From every side—are, some of them, so frail
They fuse on meeting, easily, in the air
Like gossamer or spun gold, more frail by far
Than things which catch the eye or stir the vision.
The kind of images I mean can pass

Through even the finest bodily pores, can rouse
The delicate nature of the mind within
And stimulate sensation. In this way
We look at Centaurs, Scyllas, hounds of Hell,
The images of dead men underground.
All kinds of images forever float
About us everywhere, and some are born
Of their own generation in the air
And some have more substantial origin
And some are compounds of two things or more,
For certainly no Centaur-image comes
From any single living beast; how could it?
There never was such a creature. But some chance
Might bring the images of horse and man
Together in a blend, and that would be
Easy enough to do, no great surprise,
Since images are spun so very thin.
All other things like these are fashioned so,
Supremely light, so swiftly borne along
Any one image, by one impact, moves
The mind, whose nature, as I've said before,
Is very delicate and sensitive.

I need not press the point that what we see,
Whether the eyes behold it, or the mind,
Works the same way. Suppose I see a lion:
Its image, or its sum of images,
Is making an impression on my eyes,
And if I see the idea of a lion
Or anything whatever, it's the same—
Except the mind, perhaps, has subtler power,
Perceives more tenuous images. The mind,
Wakeful, attentive, while the body sleeps,
Senses in dark those images our eyes
Derive through daylight only. So we see
Or think we see as if he were alive
Some absent prisoner of death and dust.
This is a consequence of natural law,

Because the wits are dormant when our limbs
Relax in slumber, and cannot confute
Falsehood with truth, and even memory lies
Adrowsing, with no argument to prove
Our vision error and our living man
The absent prisoner of death and dust.
And it's no marvel that these phantoms move,
Gesture, and walk, as images in dreams
Appear to do, one following another
Before the first has time to strike a pose.
They are very swift, they are very numerous,
As they would have to be, to shift and change
So quickly in such brevity of time.

There are many questions still to answer, much
To clarify, if we are serious.
We might begin by asking first of all
Why mind as soon as it takes a notion thinks
Whatever it wants to right away. Is this
Because the images regard our will,
Wait for our beck and call, and come to us
At our sweet pleasure, bringing us a sea,
An earth, a heaven? Does one word suffice
For nature to prepare, create for us
Assemblages, processions, banquets, brawls?
(Other men, to be sure, in the same place,
Have quite a different set of schemes in mind.)
What about this—that in our dreams we see
Images moving, almost keeping time,
As, softly, softly, so the left foot follows
Shadow and gesture of the right hand's lift?
Do we infer that phantoms are imbued,
Deep-dyed in art, and even though vagrant prove
Their learned discipline, abroad at night,
Indulging in their pastimes? Or is this
More probable?—that in a single time,
No longer than it takes an eye to blink
Or mouth to utter half a syllable,

Below this instant, this split-second, lie
Times almost infinite, which reason knows
As presences, and in each presence dwells
Its own peculiar image, all of them
So tenuous no mind is sharp enough
To see them all, must focus, concentrate
On only one, so all the rest are lost
Except the one mind has determined on.
Mind does prepare itself, and hopes to see,
Anticipates the next successive image,
And therefore finds it, as it must. Don't eyes,
Looking for things almost invisible,
Prepare themselves, strain, squint, and concentrate,
And only so discover what they seek?
And even in things quite obvious, your mind
Must be attentive, otherwise they'll seem
Far off in time, in space. Is it so strange
That mind keeps overlooking many things
Save those to which it pays immediate heed?
Another thing we do is fool ourselves,
Become the dupes of logic which derives
Giant conclusions out of pygmy clues.

Images may be inconsistent things.
A woman, so it seems, becomes a man
While we are watching, or an ugly one
Grows beautiful, a young one old, and so on,
While slumber and forgetfulness preserve
Our lack of challenge or of wonderment.

Another fallacy comes creeping in
Whose errors you should be meticulous
In trying to avoid—don't think our eyes,
Our bright and shining eyes, were made for us
To look ahead with; don't suppose our thigh-bones
Fitted our shin-bones, and our shins our ankles,
So that we might take steps; don't think that arms
Dangled from shoulders and branched out in hands

With fingers at their ends, both right and left,
For us to do whatever need required
For our survival. All such argument,
All such interpretation, is perverse,
Fallacious, puts the cart before the horse.
No bodily thing was born for us to use,
Nature had no such aim, but what was born
Creates the use. There could be no such thing
As sight before the eyes were formed, no speech
Before the tongue was made, but tongues began
Long before speech was uttered, and the ears
Were fashioned long before a sound was heard,
And all the organs, I feel sure, were there
Before their use developed; they could not
Evolve for the sake of use, be so designed.
But battling hand to hand, and slashing limbs,
Fouling the foe in blood—these antedate
The flight of shining javelins; nature taught
Men how to dodge a wound before they learned
The fit of shield to arm. Rest, certainly,
Is older in the history of man
Than coverlets or mattresses, and thirst
Was quenched before the days of cups or goblets.
Need has created use, as man contrives
Devices for his comfort, but all these
Cunning inventions are far different
From all those things, much older, which supplied
Their function from their form. The limbs, the sense,
Came first, their usage afterward. Never think
They could have been created for the sake
Of being used.

                    It's natural enough
That every living body looks for food,
Requires replenishment. As I have shown,
There is a constant floating-off, an ebb
From many substances in many ways,
But most of all from living animals

Since these are always moving, losing weight,
Sweating away excess, exhaling air
In sheer exhaustion, so the body thins
And all its natural strength is undermined,
Whence pain ensues, and for this reason food
Is taken, to restore the weakened limbs,
Re-create vital forces, satisfy
The appetite through muscle, vein and nerve.
And fluid sustenance also finds its way
To where there's need of fluid; fever's fires
Are quenched, the hunger and thirst are washed away,
The framework of the house is sound again.

Next we consider motion, how it is
That we can walk at will, stride boldly forth,
Propel our bulk along. Be attentive now.
I say that the first step, before we take
A step at all, is that into our mind
An image comes of walking, strikes the mind,
Creates volition; no man ever starts
To act before the mind foresees its will.
In other words, the foresight of the mind
Produces the appropriate replica,
The image; therefore, if the purpose tends
Toward the desire of going for a walk
This image or this vision strikes full force
Through all the mass of spirit, through the limbs,
The members of the body. This makes sense
If we recall how closely flesh and mind
Are linked, and so this impact on the spirit
Propels the body forward. Here we go,
Our whole mass shoved along, or moving on.
The body in motion, furthermore, expands,
Dilates, so that the air, whose property
Is always that of motion, pours in flood
Through all the openings, and is resolved,
Distributed into body's tiniest holds,
And body, like a ship, is borne along

By sails and wind. Is it so wonderful
That bodies, gross and huge, are made to move
By particles of breath, by spirit's air?
Not so, if you remember the wind's way,
How frail its substance, how invisible,
And yet how its might has power to propel
A battleship; a single steersman's hand,
Turning the wheel, can shift and swing the rush
On a new course. In the same way machines—
The winches, derricks, pulleys—lift and lower
The cargo-tons from hold to deck, to dock,
With very little strain and effort.

                          Sleep
Is our next topic, how it floods the limbs
With quietude, dispelling from the heart
The mind's anxieties. I'll try to be
Melodious at this point, and not too long,
As the swans' music pleases more than the cranes'
Squawking on their raucous course through southern clouds.
This calls, on your part, for a listening ear
And keen intelligence, lest you contradict
My argument, call it impossible,
And in your ignorance shrink in dismay
From truths you lack ability to see.
So, to begin with: sleep occurs at times
When spirit's force is somewhat discomposed
Throughout the limbs, some of it vanishing
To outer air, and some of it gone deep
Inward to crowded quarters. Then the limbs
Relax, almost dissolve. Beyond all doubt
Sensation in us has its origin
In spirit's action, and when sleep annuls
Sensation altogether, we conclude
Spirit has been disturbed, or consciousness
Driven outside the body—not, of course,
Completely so, for in that case we'd lie
Sprawled in the everlasting chill of death,

Since, if no fraction of the spirit stayed
Within our limbs, like fire beneath gray ash,
Whence could sensation suddenly blaze up,
Be blown to life, like flame from fire unseen?

Let me explain how this particular change
Takes place, how spirit is disturbed, how body
Drowses in languishment. Don't go to sleep!
Don't let me cast my lessons to the winds!
First, since the surface of the body lies
Exposed to air, it must be buffeted,
Thumped, pounded on by air's continual beat,
Against which almost everything evolves
Its own protective covering, like skin,
Or shells, or callouses, or rind, or bark.
And this same air pervades the innerpart
As we inhale, exhale; it strikes the body
Both ways at once, and as these blows persist
In penetration through the smallest pores
To our most elemental particles,
In time, and little by little, so to speak,
The limbs, beneath this constant pressure, yield,
Slump and collapse, the regular arrangement
Of particles disordered, body and mind.
So part of the spirit seems ejected, part
Driven to refuge somewhat deeper down,
Part pulled asunder from its complement,
So that reciprocal function comes to a halt
Since nature has blocked communication's lines,
And with sensation utterly out of reach,
Gone deeper down: no force holds up the limbs,
Body is weak, arms dangle at your sides,
Your eyelids droop, and on your buckling knees
You just about can stagger into bed.
A heavy meal has much the same effect
If scattered through the veins. The deepest sleep
Is that which comes when we are very tired
Or very stuffed with food; those are the times

When physical elements are most disarranged
From long exhaustion, and the spirit's power
Likewise most troubled, shattered, driven deep.

Now as for dreams: here, I suggest, we find,
Each one of us, whatever our desires
Seize and hang onto in our waking hours.
The lawyers plead in court or draw up briefs,
The generals wage wars, the mariners
Fight with their ancient enemy the wind,
And I keep doing what I am doing here:
I try to learn about the way things are
And set my findings down in Latin verse.
Oh, all the fascinations that possess
The minds of men, their studies and their arts,
Are with us in our dreaming, are, for once,
Almost attainable. Men who spend their time
Day after day at ballgames, concentrate,
Watch every move, intense, intent, still see,
In recollection, after the season ends,
The athletes leap and run; they need not be
Asleep to have such visions of the mind.
Your opera-lovers hear bright eloquence
Of song outpouring, and the orchestra
Accompany that music; they can see
The panoply of stage effect, the pause,
The sweep, the swirl, of color. What we love,
What we devote our ardor to, or seek
In passionate earnest; even what we do
In our most commonplace and daily round,
Makes all the difference, and this applies
Not only to men, but to all the animals.
Some day, in fact, you'll see a thoroughbred,
Asleep in a stall, break out in a sudden sweat,
His breath come faster and faster, and his sides
Heave as he seems to pass the winning post
Or break as the starting-gate flies open. Hounds
Twitch in their sleep, or try their best to run,

Give tongue, and sniff the air, as if they caught
Scent of their quarry. If you wake them up,
They'll chase the phantom of the stag they view
Bounding away from them, until at last
They come to learn the error of their ways,
Returning gloomy to their wiser selves
Chopfallen in their disillusionment.
Domestic dogs, or even pups, will start
Out of a dream, and shake themselves, and snarl
As if they saw a burglar in the house.
The fiercer every breed, the more it tends
To savage dreams, but the bright-colored birds
Wing through the dark, disturb the sacred groves
In panic if they dream of seeing hawks
Come swooping down to kill. The minds of men
Continue in their dreams the great pursuits
Of daytime hours—kings are victorious
Or taken prisoner, or, in torture, scream
As if their throats were being cut. Men fight,
Men groan in pain, men fill the air around
With cries, as if a panther or a lion
Were gnawing on their bones; some men discuss
Important business matters in their dreams,
Some give themselves away, and many die,
And many, hurled from mountaintops or towers
Headlong to earth, are frightened from their sleep
But, even waked, do not at once regain
Their bodily composure. A thirsty man
Sits by a river or a pleasant spring
And almost drinks it dry. Kids wet the bed
Soaking not only sheets, but also spreads,
Magnificent Babylonian counterpanes,
Because it seemed that in their dreams they stood
Before a urinal or chamber pot
With lifted nightgowns. What a lake they make!
And youngsters somewhat older, once the seed
Of manhood starts to fill their genitals,
Beholding in their dreams a lovely face,

A beautiful complexion, or a form
Desirable and fair, are so aroused,
So stirred, excited, swollen, that the deed
Becomes reality, and a tidal flow
Pours out to stain their garments.

                                 Now this seed—
Have I mentioned this before?—once we are men
Mature and strong, becomes an active force,
Compulsive, driving. Various effects
Derive from various causes, but we know
Only a human being's force can draw
The human seed from any human being.
This seed, diverse in origin, proceeds
Through all the limbs and members of the body
To its own area, where it excites
The genitals alone. These parts, aroused,
Swell with the seed, so that desire ensues
For its ejection, outpour and release,
In such direction as its craving tends.
The body seeks the source of the mind's wound.
All things tend woundward: does not blood spurt out
In the direction of the blow? is not
An enemy, standing near enough, dyed red?
So anyone, wounded by Venus' dart,
Whether it's flung by some delightful boy
With lovely girlish figure, or is cast
By a real woman, radiant with desire,
Responds in that direction, yearns and longs
And strives for union with it, wants to fill
That body with his own, pour out that seed
Into the other, and his silent lust
Anticipates that wonderful delight.

There's Venus for you! And her name supplies
Another term for love, if you must know,
The word I have in mind is *venery*—
One drop of sweetness in the heart, and then

A cold anxiety. If what you love
Is far away, no matter; images
Are there before your eyes, and the dear name
Rings in your ears. Better to run away,
Escape from such illusions, frighten off
Such things as nourish love, and turn the mind
Anywhere else, disseminate the rank
Accumulation, turn it loose, be bound
To no one frenzied appetite, with care
And pain your certain destiny. The sore
Takes on new life, persists and thrives; the madness
Worsens from day to day, its weight of pain
More burdensome; the only thing to do
Is to confuse the issue, cure the hurt
By many more—what does the adage say,
Safety in hordes? Ah, that's the right prescription.

Avoiding passionate love, you need not miss
All the rewards of Venus; you might gain
Easing and comfort without penalty.
Surely delight comes in a purer form
To sensible men than to your love-struck wretches
Who, on the very verge of consummation,
Can't make their minds up, thrash about, uncertain
Which they should pleasure first—their hands? their eyes?
So they bear down with all their weight, or squeeze,
Tight as they can, the body they have sought,
They make it hurt, take hold of lips with teeth,
Kiss with insistent fierceness. Such delight
Is never pure, for in its impulse lies
The appetite for pain, the urge to hurt,
The germinal seeds of madness. Even so,
In the very midst of love, ever so lightly,
Venus abates the punishment, and blends
A sweetness with the sharpness of the bite.
There's the hope, always, that the fire may die
Extinguished by the body which aroused
Its ardor in the first place. What could be

More contrary to nature? Nothing else
Inflames us, once we have it, with desire
Of more and more and more. We satisfy
Our hunger and our thirst with bread and wine
Whose particles have substance and can fill
Our need, can take a place within our bodies;
But pretty faces, fair complexions, bring
Nothing to body's emptiness but only
Frail, vain, elusive images, which hope
Grasps for in vain across the empty air.
In dreams, a thirsting man attempts to drink,
But finds no water which can cool the fire
Within him; therefore, all unsatisfied,
Seeks images of water, comes at last
To a rushing river, where he seems to drink
In vain, still thirsty. So it is in love.
Venus plays tricks on lovers with her game
Of images which never satisfy.
Looking at bodies fills no vital need
However nakedly the lovers gaze,
However much their hands go wandering
And still are empty—can they gather bloom
From tender limbs? And then the time arrives
When their embraces join, and they delight
In the full flower of love, or almost do,
Anticipating rapture soon to come,
The moment of the sowing. Eagerly
They press their bodies close, join lips and tongues,
Their breath comes faster, faster. All in vain,
For they can gather nothing, they cannot
Effect real penetration, be absorbed
Body in body, utterly. They seem
To want to do just this. God knows they try,
Cling to each other, lashed in Venus' chains
Till finally, all passion spent, they die,
Relaxed completely from that violence,
Melted, undone; so, for a little time,
The furious fire subsides. But it will blaze,

Break out again in madness, and they'll seek
Again whatever it is they want to reach,
Find no prescription, no device to stop
This rank infection, so they peak and pine,
Confused and troubled by their secret wound.

For this they work themselves to death, worn out,
Exhausted, spent. As if that weren't enough,
Each partner waits the other's beck and call;
Assets are spent on Eastern luxuries,
Duty is shirked, and reputation reels,
Palsied, blind-drunk. But aren't those lovely things
She's wearing?—those cute sandals on her feet,
Those great big flashing emeralds whose light
Is set in gold, that sea-dark *robe de nuit*
Worn all the time, its texture barely proof
Against love's stain and sweat. What father left
Turns into coronets or necklaces
Or an expensive lovely silken gown
From Ceos or Alinda. And it all
Adds up to nothing—banquets, rich attire,
Food, entertainment, gambling, drinks, perfumes,
Since from the fountains of delight one jet
Spurts such a bitterness the flowers wilt
All through the garden. It may be the mind
Gnaws on itself in guilt, or conscience cries
Against such indolent wanton suicide,
Or it may be some double talk of hers,
Tossed off at random, or perhaps let fly
With serious intent, has hit the mark,
Has pierced his heart and set infection there,
Or he may think she bats her eyes too much
In some one else's presence, looks too fond,
And that her subtle and beguiling smile
Means she is laughing at him.

                                    Griefs like these
Are common enough when things are going well

And happily, as we say. When things are rough,
Griefs multiply to such infinities
Your eyes, tight shut, can see them. Be on guard,
As I have taught you, don't be taken in.
It's easier to avoid the snares of love
Than to escape once you are in that net
Whose cords and knots are strong; but even so,
Enmeshed, entangled, you can still get out
Unless, poor fool, you stand in your own way,
Forgetting, for example, all those faults
Your little darling has in body or mind.
Desire is blind, desire is ignorant,
And men can never stop this foolishness
But keep on praising an attractive charm
Which simply isn't there. We often see
The crookedest and ugliest woman held
In high esteem, somebody's precious pet;
And some men laugh at others, urging them
To placate Venus, have her intervene,
Ease the affliction of so foul a mess,
And yet these wretches never understand
Their own calamitous cases. A black wench
Is a nut-brown maid, and some untidy slob
Praised for a sweet disorder in the dress.
Some idiot with a pallid washed-out stare
Is called grey-eyed Minerva, olive-groved.
The lumbering lummox is a wood nymph wild,
The sawed-off runt a doll, the overgrown
Hydrocephalic is divinely tall
And walks the night in beauty—(a good thing, too;
Keep her locked up by day.) That speech defect
Turns out to be the thweetetht little lithp,
The one too dumb to say a single word
Is shy and modest, while the gabby gawk
Who never stops talking, flings herself around
All over the place—who can this Sylvia be
Except the life of the party? Miss Flat Chest
Is slender-slim as willow-wands or briony;

The bulging blown-up over-bosomy babe
Is the Earth-Mother; and the hairy snub-nose,
Cute little monkey-face. The catalogue
Is much too long for us to itemize.
Concede her face all glory, laud, and honor,
Concede that every muscle, every nerve
In her entire anatomy, responds
To Venus' music—aren't there other girls?
Didn't you get along for quite some time
Without her? Her performances, we know,
Are just the same as uglier women's are,
So she pours on perfumery so rank
It almost suffocates her serving maids
Who get away from her as far as they can,
Or titter, behind her back, across the room.
Meanwhile her dear devoted lover-man,
Shut out of the house, is weeping bitter tears,
Piling the threshold deep with flowers and wreaths,
Making the doorposts sticky with his kisses.
Suppose, though, he's let in, and gets one whiff,
Only one single whiff, of that bouquet.
If he has any decency at all,
He ought to find some reason, some excuse
For an abrupt departure, sigh no more
Those heartfelt and interminable blues,
But recognize his own damn foolishness:
This creature on her silly pedestal
Is not a goddess! All our Venuses
Are well aware of this; so, all the more,
They try to hide their backstage scenery
From those romantic swains they hope to keep
Held tight and handcuffed in love's manacles.
A fatuous project. All you have to do
Is use a little wit and bring to light
All this ridiculous nonsense. If, in turn,
She shows a decent spirit, holds no grudge,
You might as well forget it. Aren't we all
Human and fallible?

When a woman joins
Body to body in a tight embrace,
Moist-kissing lip to lip, breathes deep, or sighs
That long-drawn sigh, this is no act of fraud,
No simulated passion; many times
She means it absolutely, from the depths,
Desires the satisfactions both can share,
Urging him to his utmost. Animals
Act the same way, the tame ones and the wild,
Birds in the mating season, mares in heat,
The female more than willing for the male
To tread or mount; and in their bonds of love
You see the partners thrash and struggle, bound
In what—delight or torment? Look at dogs
Caught back to back, about to cross a street,
Where each tries hard to go a different way,
Unable to separate. Why do things like this?
There ought to be a two-way pleasure to it.
I have said this over and over, many times.

When the male seed and female seed are fused,
One partner may be dominant, overpower
The other in a burst of violence.
If this should be the woman, then the child
Will have her features and her qualities.
The same thing happens if the man assumes
The role of dominance, the children then
Will be more like the father. When you see
Daughters and sons whose build and looks appear
The heritage of both alike, be sure
That in the act of procreative love
A parity existed, neither one
Being lord or slave, victim or conqueror.
At times, again, resemblances can skip
A generation or more, and reproduce
A distant ancestor. The cause of this
Lies in the fact that hidden in all bodies
Are many first-beginnings, primal motes

Passed on by the successive generations,
And out of these the goddess fashions forms
Whose lot is various, on a child bestows
Ancestral traits of voice, complexion, hair.
Sons may be like their mothers, and the girls
More like their fathers; this is natural
Since all things born are made from double seed,
Although in mixed proportion; this is clear
Whatever the sex of the new generation.

As for sterility, no gods inflict
This curse on men who never get a child
To call them father, who expend their days
In barren intercourse, and in their gloom
Think that the gods must be responsible—
And so they sprinkle altar stones with blood
And make them reek with incense or the smoke
Of their burnt-offerings, and pray for wives
Made pregnant by the rivers of their seed.
How futile and how tiresome this must be
To any god's caprice or will! The fault
Lies in the seed itself, too thick, too thin.
The latter has no clinging force, dissolves,
Declares itself abortive, while the thick,
Being too clogged, too clotted, cannot spurt
With any truly pentrative force;
And even if it finally arrives
At where it should, its power, completely spent,
Cannot be mingled with the female seed.

Love's concords may be very different,
Some men more efficacious with some women,
Some women more surely pregnant by some men,
And many women, whose first marriages
Were barren, later come to other husbands
To whom they bear a goodly store of offspring,
A sweet delight. And late in life, some husbands
Whose wives, though far from barren, never bore

Children in that particular house, have found
A different partner, better suited for them,
An old age blessed with sons. The seeds must be
Compatible, adapted to each other,
Thick compensating thin, and coarse with fine
Effecting harmony. Diet also plays
A most important role; some foods condense
The seed, some thin it down to almost nothing.
And posture, in the very act of love,
Must not be disregarded; it is thought
Women conceive more readily, if taken
As animals are, breasts underneath, loins high,
So that the seed reaches the proper parts
More readily. Wives have no need at all
For loose and limber motions, pelvic stunts,
Abdominal gyrations. These, in fact,
Are contraceptive; if she pulls away,
Pretends reluctance, stirs him up again
With strain and push and thrusting, she diverts
The seed from its right furrow. This is why
All whores are so gymnastic; they know well
Such acts not only please their customers
But also are a safeguard, good insurance
Against a pregnant belly. But our wives,
It seems, need no such nonsense. Finally,
The little woman does not have to be
A raving beauty; she can win your love,
Without the help of any gods, without
The darts of Cupids or of Venuses,
Simply by being decent, neat and clean,
A pleasant person to be living with.
That's about all it takes, and love depends
On habit quite as much as the wild ways
Of passion. Gently does it, as the rain
In time wears through the very hardest stone.

Book V

Whose genius has the power to utter song
Fit for the grandeur of the way things are,
For these discoveries? Who has the strength
In words to fashion any adequate praise
For what that man deserves, whose intellect
Found and bequeathed us such a store of wealth?
No one of us, no son of mortal stock,
Will ever, I'd guess, rise to the majesty
Required to praise such greatness. Ah, my friend,
Most noble Memmius, we must admit
He was a god, a god indeed, who first
Found a life-scheme, a system, a design
Now known as Wisdom, or Philosophy.
He was the one whose artistry brought life
Out of the turbulence, the darknesses,
Into serenity and shining light.
Compare with his those other ancient gifts
Attributed to gods: Ceres, we say,
Gave grain to men, and Bacchus brought us wine,
But life, without these gifts, is possible—
Some races do without them even today
And do not suffer. But there's no good life,
No blessedness, without a mind made clear,
A spirit purged of error. So all the more
He seems to us, by absolute right, a god
From whom, distributed through all the world,
Come those dear consolations of the mind,
That precious balm of spirit. If you think
The feats of Hercules compare with his,

You'll wander in error, almost out of your mind.
How could that gap-mouth, the Nemean lion,
Harm us today? What could the bristly boar
From Arcady do, or the Cretan bull, or the freak
Of Lerna, ruffed with poisonous snakes, accomplish?
Of what avail Geryon's triple menace,
Bronze-plumed Stymphalian marsh birds, or the fire
Blown out by Diomed's horses? And that dragon,
Glowering fierce and huge, coiled round a treetrunk,
Guarding the golden apples of the west
By the Atlantic's merciless rage of rock
And shore—how could he damage us? We never
Go there, not one of us; neither do strangers,
Barbarians, folk uncivilized. They dare not.
As for the other dreadful presences
Slaughtered by Hercules, let us suppose
They never were brought low; what difference
Would it have made, what harm accrue, if they
Were living still? Not much, or none at all,
I'd say—a drop in the bucket, hardly more.
For the world even now is full to the brim
With savage creatures; terror and panic haunt
The mountains, forests, jungles, but at least
We have an excellent chance of staying home,
Of never touring any such demesnes.
But if the reason is unpurified,
The conscious mind unpurged, what wars we wage
Within ourselves, what dangers penetrate
Against our will! How many fierce desires
Slash into our anxiety! What fears
Ensue, what nastiness, what arrogance,
Pride, self-indulgence, lust, sloth, graspingness,
Disaster-bringers all! And so the man
Who conquered all of these and by his words
Rather than by arms expelled them from the mind
Must be, if decency has any force,
Accorded rank and worth with any god,

Especially, since like a god he spoke
With lofty eloquence about the gods,
About the way things are.

                                    I tread the path
Where he has led, I teach, I tell, what laws
Hold all created things, how bound they are
To an endurance of order, cannot break,
Cannot rescind the legislation Time
Has fixed forever. A first principle,
By way of illustration: I have shown
That mind, or soul, by nature, has been proved
To be a property of mortal stuff,
Unable to endure unharmed forever;
And when we see, or think we see, in dreams
A man whom death has taken, we are fooled
By vain delusive images. I must
Continue now, must show that all the world
Is mortal also, I must show the ways
Whereby, when elements of matter met,
Their union founded earth, sky, sea, stars, sun,
The lunar globe. And I must also tell
What animals have existed on the earth,
And what ones never lived at any time;
How, by their varied utterance and tone,
Men could communicate by naming things;
How fear of the gods crept into human hearts,
Imposing over all the world dread awe
Of the holy lakes, groves, altars, images.
Beyond this, I'll explain the power whereby
With nature at the helm, the sun and moon
Are steered along their courses, lest we think
They make their annual processionals
At their own whim between the earth and sky
Indulgently promoting the increase
Of crops and animals, or perhaps are whirled

By some caprice or purpose of the gods.
Students, even those who have learned the lesson well
That gods lead lives supremely free of care,
May wonder now and then by what intent
This thing or that can happen, most of all
In areas overhead. This wonderment
Leads to confusion, leads them to regress
To obsolete religious awe, to invoke
A bitter lordship for themselves (poor fools)
Believers in almighty gods, and blind,
Credulous, ignorant of what can be
And what cannot, limits and boundaries—
The deep-set marker that is fixed forever.
I keep you waiting with my promises;
We'd best be getting on. Now, Memmius,
Look at the seas, the lands, the sky. All these,
With their three-fold diversity of form,
Of nature, fabric, mass, one day will bring
To ruin utterly; and all that might,
All that machinery of the universe,
Upheld so proudly through so many years,
Will tumble down, crumble to ruin, die.
I have no doubt how strange and new the mind
Finds the idea that heaven and earth are doomed.
How hard for any words of mine to prove!
It's like this always, isn't it, when you bring
Something the ears have never heard before
And eyes can't visualize, or fingers grasp,
Where only the paved highway of belief
Is the short boulevard to heart and mind?
But even so, I shall speak out. My words,
Perhaps, will be confirmed by actual fact,
And you will see, in just a little while,
Tremendous earthquakes, universal shock.
May Fortune, at the helm, steer far from us
Any such wrack, and may we rather learn
By reason, not experience, the truth

That all the universe can be struck down,
Disintegrate, in horrible rumble and crash.

Before I play Sir Oracle, and speak
With sounder sense than any priestess ever
Gave out from Phoebus' tripod and his laurel,
Let me first bring you more than a little comfort
In learnèd words; for I'd not have you be
So superstitious, snaffled, as to think
The earth and sun and sky, sea, stars, and moon
Are made of stuff divine, and live forever.
Next thing you know, you'll think it right and proper
That what the Giants suffered for their crimes,
For their monstrosities, applies as well
To all those men whose powers of reason shatter
The barriers of the universe, who would
Darken the sunlight in their arrogance,
Marking with mortal talk immortal things.
But as a matter of fact, such things are far
From any aura of divinity,
From any semblance of godly character,
And should be, rather, taken as good proof
Of something lacking vital, sensitive movement.
It simply isn't so, that everything
Which has a body also has a mind,
An aim in life, a planned curriculum.
Trees don't live in the sky, and clouds don't swim
In the salt seas, and fish don't leap in wheatfields,
Blood isn't found in wood, nor sap in rocks.
By fixed arrangement, all that lives and grows
Submits to limit and restriction. So
Mind must derive from body, mind can never
Be far from blood and sinew. But if mind
(And this would be more likely) could exist
In one location only, say the head,
Or shoulders, or the bottom of the heels,
Even so, its residence would have to be
In the same man, that is to say, the same

Containing vessel. It is obvious
Our bodily arrangement and disposal
Sets limits to the areas which mind
Can occupy; so, all the more, we must
Deny that somewhere, out beyond animal form
Or animal substance, mind is ever found
In crumbling clods of earth, in the sun's fire,
In water, in the lofty seas of air.
Such things as these, therefore, are not endowed
With any sentience, least of all divine.
They are not even living.

                    One more thing
You can't believe: that the gods dwell somewhere
In hallowed places in our universe.
Not so: gods' natures are impalpable,
Far from our senses' range, hardly perceptible
By the mind's eye; our hands cannot reach out
To touch them, therefore, being intangible,
They cannot touch us either—touch, of course,
Being reciprocal. So their abodes
Must be unlike our own, as tenuous
As it may be their bodies are; the proof
Of this, a rather lengthy argument,
I'll give you later. Meanwhile, let's not be
So foolish as to say that for men's sake
The gods were more than willing to prepare
The gorgeous structure of the universe,
Which therefore, as the work of gods, must be
Considered laudable, and as their work
Immortal also—what a sinful thing
(We think) for such a world, established by
The ancient planning of the gods for men,
To be subverted, ever, from its base
By any violence, subject to storms
Of sacrilegious verbiage, overthrown,
Brought low, brought down, destroyed, annihilated,
And so forth, and so on. All nonsense, Memmius!

What could the blessèd, the immortal, gain
From any such munificence as ours
To tackle anything for our sweet sake?
What novelty could so distract, so break
Their eons-long serenity and rouse
Their willingness to change their ancient ways?
Those whom the old things vex are right, of course,
To find delight in new ones; but suppose
You had no trouble in all your days, enjoyed
A life of utter bliss, what in the world
Could make you burn for novelty? The gods
Lived, I suppose, in darkness and in grief
Until illumined by their handiwork,
The world's creation? How would we be hurt
If we were never born? Once given life,
We want to keep on living, anyway
As long as there is any pleasure in it;
But if a man has never had a taste
Of life, or never had his name put down
In the catalogue of those who loved it, how,
How could nonbeing do him any harm?
Furthermore, where would the gods derive a scheme
For making things, how would they understand
What men were to be like, so gods could know,
Or only imagine, how to fashion them?
Or how would they comprehend the principles
Of primal bodies, what was possible
Through changed arrangements, unless nature gave
A model for creation? Atoms move
In many ways, since infinite time began,
Are driven by collisions, are borne on
By their own weight; in every kind of way
Meet or combine, try every possible,
Every conceivable pattern, so no wonder
They fell into arrangements, into modes
Like those whereby the sum of things preserves
Its system by renewal.

But suppose
That I were ignorant and did not know
What atoms are, I'd still make bold a claim
To state, from my observance of the ways
Of heaven, and from many other things:
This world of ours was not prepared for us
By any god. Too much is wrong with it.
For one thing, what the mighty swirl of sky
Protects, the covetous mountains and the jungles
Have seized a part of, and the cliffs and swamplands
Appropriate their share; and then there's ocean
Keeping the shores as wide apart as may be.
Two-thirds of what there is, that pair of thieves,
Fierce heat, insistent cold, have robbed men of;
And what is left, nature, as violent
As either one, would occupy and homestead
With fence of briar and bramble, but men resist
For their dear lives, groan as they heave the mattock
The way they know they must, or break the soil
Shoving the plow along. Were this not done,
This plowshare-turning of the fertile clod,
This summoning to birth, nothing at all
Could, of its own initiative, leap forth
Into the flow of air. How many a time
The produce of great agonies of toil
Burgeons and flourishes, and then the sun
Is much too hot and burns it to a crisp;
Or sudden cloudbursts, zero frosts, or winds
Of hurricane force are, all of them, destroyers.
And why does nature feed and multiply
The dreadful race of predatory beasts,
Man's enemies on sea and land? And why
Must every season bring disease? And why
Is early death so free to walk the world?
When nature, after struggle, tears the child
Out of its mother's womb to the shores of light,
He lies there naked, lacking everything,

Like a sailor driven wave-battered to some coast,
And the poor little thing fills all the air
With lamentation—but that's only right
In view of all the griefs that lie ahead
Along his way through life. The animals
Are better off, the tame ones and the wild,
They grow, they don't need rattles, they don't need
The babbling baby-talk of doting nurses,
They don't go seeking different kinds of dress
According to the season, they don't need
Weapons or walls for their protection; earth
And nature, generous artificer,
Supply their every lack.

               What a digression!
Forgive my rambling, Memmius. My theme
Is, still, mortality: since earth and water
Air and fire, those elements which form
The sum of things are, all of them, composed
Of matter that is born and dies, we must
Conclude that likewise all the universe
Must be of mortal nature. Any time
We see that parts are transient substances
We know their total is as fugitive,
And when the main components of the world
Exhaust themselves or come to birth again
Before our very eyes, we may be sure
That heaven and earth will end, as certainly
As ever they once began.

               Do not suppose
I take too much for granted when I claim
That earth and fire are mortal, and that air
And water perish and are born again.
Take, to begin with, any part of the earth,
Burnt by continual suns, trampled by hosts,
Exhaling mist or dust, and flying clouds
Dispersed by the great gales across the sky.

Part of the soil the heavy rainstorms call
To dissolution; riverbanks are shorn,
Gnawed by the currents. For every benefit
Requital must be given. Earth's our mother,
Also our common grave. And so you see
Earth is receiving loss and gain forever.

No need for words to prove that ocean, streams,
And springs brim over always with new floods;
On every side downrushing mighty waters
Proclaim the fact, but from the surfaces
There's always a subtraction, so excess
Is nullified, wind and sun exert their powers
Of diminution, there's a seepage down
Into the earth, the salt is filtered out,
The substance of the water oozes back
To a confluence at the fountainheads
Of all the rivers, and then flows again
Down the fresh channels of its earlier days.

And air is changed completely, hour by hour,
Moment by moment, in more ways than men
Can ever count; whatever streams from things
Is always poured into that mighty sea,
The ocean of the air; but in its turn
This reassigns to things their particles
Renews them as they flow away. All things
Would otherwise by dissolved and changed to air.
There is no end to the continual process,
Air always rising out of things, and falling
Back into things again. In other words,
Recurring influence and effluence.

Likewise the generous giver of clear light,
The ethereal sun, forever flooding heaven
With new illumination, light on light,
Changed every single moment—brightness falls
From air, is lost, renewed. This you can tell

By the way clouds begin to veil the sun,
To break, as it were, the rays of light; at once
The lower part of these is gone, the earth
Is dark with shadow where the clouds ride over.
And so, you realize, things forever need
Renewal of shining, every flash of light
Loses intensity, there would be nothing
Visible in the day, did not the sun
Forever stream replenishment. Look about you!
By night we have in our own halls on earth
Our suns, such as they are, the hanging lamps,
The torches flaring bright, or thick with smoke.
What eager servants, always on the go
To keep the light renewed, the wavering flame
Uninterrupted (or at least to seem so),
With spark so quick to follow the extinction
Of prior spark! So sun and moon and stars
We know form the processional of light
In infinite new succession, a mote, a flash,
Another and another, on and on.
But don't believe none of them ever falters.

You see that stones are worn away by time,
Rocks rot, and towers topple, even the shrines
And images of the gods grow very tired,
Develop cracks or wrinkles, their holy wills
Unable to extend their fated term,
To litigate against the Laws of Nature.
And don't we see the monuments of men
Collapse, as if to ask us, "Are not we
As frail as those whom we commemorate?"?
Boulders come plunging down from mountain heights,
Poor weaklings, with no power to resist
The thrust that says to them, *Your time has come!*
But they would be rooted in steadfastness
Had they endured from time beyond all time,
As far back as infinity. Look about you!
Whatever it is that holds in its embrace

All earth, if it projects, as some men say,
All things out of itself, and takes them back
When they have perished, must itself consist
Of mortal elements. The parts must add
Up to the sum. Whatever gives away
Must lose in the procedure, and gain again
Whenever it takes back.

                           But let's suppose
There never was any primogeniture
For earth and sky, but they were always there,
Always existing—could not poets find
In such potential annals ancient lays,
Much earlier matter to be singing of,
Before the Seven Against, or the Fall of Troy?
How could so many deeds of so many heroes
Fade into so much dark oblivion
Without one blossom of memorial?
No, no; our world, I think, is very young,
Has hardly more than started; some of our arts
Are in the polishing stage, and some are still
In the early phases of their growth; we see
Novel equipment on our ships, we hear
New sounds in our music, new philosophies—
How recent the discovery of the scheme,
The system of the universe, which I
Am actually the first one to express
In our own mother tongue! But if you think
That all these things were once the very same,
Long generations past, that humankind
Died out in tropic heat, or cities fell
In some gigantic temblor of the world,
Or that the rivers, deluge-swollen, surged
Over the earth to swallow up the towns,
Then, all the more, you must confess you lose
The argument, you must admit that doom
Some day will come upon our earth, our sky.
For with such peril and pestilence abroad

Assailing things, if there had only been
The addition of a fiercer violence,
Perhaps not even very much, the world
Would have come down in utter wrack and ruin;
And for sure proof that we ourselves are mortal,
We see our kind fall sick of the same diseases
That other men have died of.

                          Furthermore,
For things to be eternal, they should have
A nature absolutely firm and solid
To bounce blows off, let nothing penetrate
With power to shatter close-packed particles,
As are those motes of matter we described
A while ago. Or, things might last forever
Because no blow can touch them, being void,
Or else because they have no space around them
Into which elements might pass, or be
Dissoluble. The total quantity
Of all the sums must be immutable
And everlasting, with no space beyond
Where fractions leap apart, no area
Whence shattering impacts might originate.
But I have shown the nature of the world
Is dual, void and solid, emptiness
Combined with matter, no such emptiness
That bodily forms can never penetrate
With almost whirlwind violence and impose
Doom and destruction. There is never lack
Of outer space, available to take
The exploded rampart-rubble of the world.
The doors of death are always open wide:
For sky, for sun, for earth, for ocean's deeps
The vast and gaping emptiness lies in wait.
So you must grant that once upon a time
Such things as these were born; no mortal things
Could have endured, from earlier than forever,
The overwhelming dominance of time,
Of time unbounded.

With the elements
Fighting their fierce and fratricidal wars,
Can't you imagine there will be some day
An ultimate truce? Either the heat of the sun
Will dry up all the rivers—this indeed
Is what even now that fiery force intends
But has not yet been able to accomplish
With all its trying, for the waters marshal
Their armies of reserves, not for defense
But for deliberate attack, a threat
To overwhelm the universe with flood;
But this is silly, for the sweeping winds
Abate the water, and the sun in heaven,
Their ally, makes it shrink; sun and wind
Are confident they can dry up the world
Before the water drowns it in a deluge.
So the war-breathers seek supremacy
In undecisive conflict; fire was once
Victorious, or so the story goes,
And water, at another time, was lord.
Fire was triumphant over all the world
When the sun's horses whirled poor Phaethon
All over the sky, and much too close to earth,
Till the Almighty Father, in a rage,
Struck our young hero with his thunderbolt
And blasted him from chariot to earth,
Where, as he fell, the sun-god caught the torch,
Resumed the car of light, repaired the reins,
Patted the steeds from panic into calm,
Yoked them once more, drove the familiar course
With everything in order once again.
Such is the story old Greek poets sang,
A myth, of course, quite senseless and untrue,
For fire can win only when motes of fire
Attain to almost infinite multitude,
Beyond all normal count. But even so
Their force is somehow spent; it has to be,
Or the whole world would die in holocaust.
Water once also had its day, or so

Legend relates, and poured its floods across
The cities of mankind, but that attack
At last was beaten back, we know not how,
And rainfall ceased, and rivers lost their rage.

Now I'll describe how the chaotic motes,
The turbulent atoms, met, somehow to form
The basic order of the earth, the sky,
The deep, the courses of the sun and moon.
Never suppose the atoms had a plan,
Nor with a wise intelligence imposed
An order on themselves, nor in some pact
Agreed what movements each should generate.
No, it was all fortuitous; for years,
For centuries, for eons, all those motes
In infinite varieties of ways
Have always moved, since infinite time began,
Are driven by collisions, are borne on
By their own weight, in every kind of way
Meet and combine, try every possible,
Every conceivable pattern, till at length
Experiment culminates in that array
Which makes great things begin: the earth, the sky,
The ocean, and the race of living creatures.
No sun with lavish light was visible then
Wheeling aloft, no planets, ocean, sky,
No earth, no air, no thing like things we know,
But a strange kind of turbulence, a swarm
Of first beginnings, whose discordances
Confused their intervals, connections, ways
And weights and impacts, motions and collisions;
And so the battles raged, because these forms
Were so dissimilar, so various
They could not rest in harmony, nor combine
In any reciprocal movements. But at last
Some parts began to learn their separate ways—
Like elements joined with like, in some such way
As to effect disclosure—a visible universe

With parts arranged in order, as the earth
Was sundered from the lofty sky, as ocean
Spread with its waters kept in proper bounds,
As the pure fires of heaven knew their place.

At first, no doubt of it, the bodies of earth,
Being heavy and thick-matted with each other,
Met in the middle, took the lowest places
And as they came together and adhered
More tightly, they squeezed out those particles
Which formed the sea, the stars, the sun, the moon,
The walls of the world, for every one of these
Was made of elements more smooth and round,
Much tinier than motes of earth. So ether—
Wherever there might be openings in the mesh—
Found its way upward, and its lightness trailed
Fire as it rose. In just this way we see
In morning's ruddy sunlight over lawns
Jewelled with dew the veils of mist arising
From pool or river, and it seems to us
The earth is almost smoking. All this air,
Ascending frail, thickens aloft, and weaves
A canopy of cloud across the sky.
So, long ago, the light diffusible ether
In compact circular denseness curved its way
In all directions, spread abroad, and held
All other things in its embracing fold.
Then sun and moon were born, and went their rounds
Between the earth and sky, with neither earth
Nor sky appropriating either sphere.
They were not heavy enough to sink and settle
Into the earth, nor light enough to float
Up to the ether, but their course was set
Between the two; between the two they turn
Like living bodies, their existence keeping
A time, a place, as parts of the great world.
Their motion and their fixity resemble
Our own in this respect: that we can move

Some of our bodily members while the rest
Remain in quietude.

When sun and moon
Departed, earth sank suddenly, where now
The blue-green reach of sea extends; earth's hollows
Filled with salt water, and day after day
The more the tidal force of air, the rays
Of sun beat down on earth with frequent blows,
Compressing it from width to narrowness,
Its nature all compact, so much the more
By the salt sweat exuded from its body
Its ooze increased the sea, the swimming plains;
And, likewise all the more, uncounted motes
Of heat and air escaped, rose far from earth,
Crowded the shining reaches of the sky,
Valleys and plains subsided, mountains loomed
To lofty heights, for the crags could not sink down
Nor all the parts descend to equal depth.

So, then, the weight of earth solidified,
And all the heavy sludge of all the world
Settled like lees or wine-dregs in a cask.
Then sea, then air, then all the fiery realm
Of ether, with translucent particles,
Was purified, lightnesses varying
From lightnesses, till the most delicate
Floated, most frail, above the highest breath
Of the least air, above all whirlwind force,
Unmingling with all turbulence of storm,
Smoothly the calm direction of its fire
Gliding along, like to the Pontic sea
Keeping the even tenor of its way.

For earth to rest in the middle of that realm
We call the universe, its weight must be
Diminished little by little, must decrease,
Must have some other substance underneath

Joined with it from the start, must have, above,
Some other, forming one organic whole.
This neither hinders nor depresses air
Any more than a man's limbs weigh him down, or his head
Is an overload to his neck, any more than we feel
Our whole weight bearing down upon our insoles;
Whereas any foreign matter, imposed from without,
Is a vexatious nuisance, however small
Its actual heft may be. The difference lies
In the innate capacity of things.
So earth is not some foreign body, thrust
All of a sudden on resentful air,
But from the outset of the universe
An integral part thereof, as surely so
As our own limbs and organs seem to us.
When the earth shudders at some cataclysm,
The atmosphere above is also shaken,
And this could not ensue unless the earth
Were somehow fastened and bound to air and sky.
They are joined, they cling together by common roots,
They have always been so joined and so united.
You've seen the like in the way the spirit's essence,
Frail and invisible, sustains the weight
Of our bodies, however heavy they may be.
They have always been so joined and so united.
What else but power of spirit lifts the body
Of the high-jumper up and over the bar?
By now you do see, don't you, how a frail
Nature can be most powerful, conjoined
With a substantial body, as the air
Combines with earth, as our own power of mind
Joins with our physical natures?

                              Now we turn
To sing of stellar motion. The great flow
Of heaven, as air turning, possibly may press
Each polar axis of our atmosphere
Holding it close both ways, with another stream

Of air in flow above it, setting course
In one direction only, with the stars
Revolving, shining, swept along that flood.
Or there may be another air below
To make the arc revolve the other way
As rivers turn the wheels of water-scoops.
It's also possible that all the sky
Is fixed in one position, while the stars
Pursue their shining ways. The tides of ether
May be shut in, over-compressed, revolve
Seeking escape, and whirl the fiery stars
To the Night-Thunderer's areas of sky.
Possibly, too, air currents from without
Propel the stars along; or they may graze
Of their own will, in search of nourishment
Across their meadows. It is very hard
To say what happens in this world of theirs.
I do point out what may or can be done
In all the universes of the world,
Suggesting varied theories; one of these
Must be the right one, and its force applies
To our own earth as well as starry spheres;
But no one, plodding forward step by step,
As I do, dares to say which one is true.

The sun must be as large, as hot, as it
Appears to us, no more, no less. When fire
Casts light or heat, no matter how far away,
No diminution of its mass ensues,
The firelight seems no narrower to the gaze.
So, since our senses feel the flooding heat
Of sunlight's comforting appearances,
Our apprehensions of that form and size
Must be correct; there's nothing you can add,
Nothing subtract. The same way with the moon—
Whether its light is borrowed or derived
From its own substance, makes no difference—
The moon can be no larger than it seems

To our watching eyes. Whatever we see, far off,
Is blurred before it shrinks. And so the moon
Affording us an outline sharp and clear
Must have the same dimensions in the sky
As we down here observe. No fire on earth
As long as we can sense its burning, see
The brightness of its wavering, seems to change
Appreciably in size, so all those fires
Of upper air, the stars, can hardly be
Much less or greater than they seem to us,
Or only a little, one way or the other.

And it's not too surprising that the sun,
So small a body, really, can pour out
Such copious light, enough to flood the lands,
The seas, the heavens, to warm the whole wide world.
One explanation is that through the sun
Pours one great universal flow of light
Because all cosmic particles of warmth
Foregather here for confluence, emerge
In one vast flow from one tremendous source
In the same way you've seen some small spring's issue
Irrigate meadows with wide overflow.
It's also possible that the sun itself
Is not so very hot, but aid may be—
Under the right conditions—kindling, tinder,
Like beds of thatch or straw, fired by one spark,
Or the high-shining, ruddy-lanterned sun
May have about him a great field of fire
Whose particles we cannot see revealed
By any gleam, but whose intensive powers
Greatly increase the impact of his rays.

Nor can one single simple answer give
The explanation of his annual round
From summer regions south to Capricorn
Then north again to Cancer; why does the moon
Apparently traverse in a month of time

An area that takes the sun a year?
Let me repeat—there's no one simple answer.
Democritus, that hero of the mind,
Whose judgment we revere, may well have come
As close as any one, his argument
Being that when the stars are nearer earth
They are bound to move more slowly, cannot race
With sky's full whirlwind sweep, whose force dies down,
Whose impetus slows, in lower atmosphere.
And so the zodiac-signs behind the sun
Catch up and overtake him, since his course
Is so much lower. The same way with the moon
Or even more so; farther from the sky,
Nearer the earth, by that much less her speed,
By that much less her power to match the pace
Of the zodiac signs; she moves below the sun
With weaker whirling, and it seems almost
That she is going backward, as those signs
Come sweeping by her.

                    Now here's something else—
The winds at times may flow across the path
Of the sun's journey, at right angles to it
Alternately, to shove him winterward
From Leo and the Virgin, or bring him back
From the cold shadows to the summer blaze.
And moon and stars, in the same fashion, wheeling
For eons in great orbits, also move
Driven by alternate currents of the air.
Cloud-layers, over or under each other, drift
In opposite directions, as the wind
Moves on their level; so the planets ride
Contrary currents through the arcs of ether.

Why does night darken earth? Because the sun
Has reached the farthest limits of the sky,
Is tired, breathes out his last exhausted fires,
Weakened by too much travel through the air,

Or because that same force which drove him on
Above the world now keeps him under it.

Likewise, at a fixed time, the rosy light
Of the Dawn-goddess streams through earth and air
Either because the sun comes back again
From under earth, trying to reach ahead
To light the sky with beams, or else because
Fires come together, and the seeds of flame
At a fixed time will always coalesce
Forming new suns. People around Mt. Ida
Say they have witnessed this phenomenon,
Fire-fragments first, beheld in the rising light,
Then massed together, forming a great ball.
This should not seem too wonderful, that seeds
Of fire can fuse at a fixed time, restoring
The brightness of the sun. We have instances:
At a fixed time the flowers bloom—the petals
At a fixed time fall. At a fixed time, with age,
Our teeth drop out, as earlier, with youth,
Our beards and body-hair began to grow.
Finally, lightning, snow, rain, clouds, and winds
Occur predictably, or nearly so.
When patterns are established more or less,
Even from the beginning of the world,
They tend to keep that order and recurrence.

Days lengthen, nights grow short; or the other way.
This is because the sun, above the earth
Or under it, parts the regions of the air
With curves that are not equal, breaks his round
Into uneven sectors, gives one part
What he has taken from the other side
Until he comes to a signpost in the sky
Which marks the point where day and night are equal
Exactly halfway between north and south
As the astronomers have well established.
Possibly air is denser in certain parts,

So, under earth, the tremulous crest of fire
Holds back, can't easily penetrate nor rise,
Hence the long nights of wintertime drag on
Until day's radiant banner streams again.
Or maybe at alternate seasons of the year
The fusion of the sun-producing flames
Moves at a different rate, and it's the truth
That every day a brand-new sun is born.

The moon may shine by sun's reflected light
And day by day she turns more light on us
As she draws farther and farther away from the sun.
Directly opposite the sun her light
Is fullest, as her rise beholds him set,
Then little by little she must wane and darken
As she draws nearer to him; so folk say
Who think the moon is round, a satellite
To the sun's course. She might perhaps revolve
With her own light, yet vary in her brightness
Were there some other body gliding with her,
An interfering presence, robed in darkness,
Therefore invisible. But if the moon
Is a revolving ball, one half may be
Dyed with most dazzling light, and in the turning
We have a great variety of phases
Until that hemisphere flashes at its full
Across our sight; then little by little we get
The luminous globe's slow-waning, slow-withdrawal.
Astrologists, unlike astronomers,
Insist this theory is correct; can both
Be right, I wonder? Why should we believe
One rather than another? For that matter,
Might there not be with every single day
A new moon following the one before
With a succession of forms—a vanishing,
A reappearance? This I doubt that words
Or logic can refute, since many things
Conform to a processional of order.

Spring comes, and Venus comes; ahead of them
Steps Venus' wingèd herald-boy, and Zephyr
Not far behind, as mother Flora strews
The path with blooms of every scent and hue.
Then comes dry Summer-heat, and at his side
Ceres, all dusty, and the Winnowers,
Northeasterlies, whom sunburnt Autumn follows,
Bacchus in step beside him—in their train
A following of other Storms and Winds:
Deep-thundering Volturnus, Auster, lord
Of lightning, till the Shortest-day brings snow,
And Winter the rigidity of ice,
While Chill, with teeth a-chatter, brings up the rear.
So is it any wonder, if a moon
Is born one certain day, and killed another,
Whenever so many instances arise
Based on a definite fixity of season?

As for eclipses of the sun and moon
You'd best assume there may be various causes.
Why should the moon shut sunlight from the earth
Looming before the sun with interference,
Her darkness blotting out his fiery beams?
Why is it not at least as probable
That some other body, with no light at all,
Is doing the same thing at the same time?
And who's to say the sun cannot grow tired,
Withhold his blaze at some fixed interval
And then renew his light, when he has passed
Through arcs inimical, which kill his fires?
And why can earth, in turn, deprive the moon
Of light, or in the darkness stifle sun
While, on her monthly orbiting, the moon
Rides through and over the long conic shadow?
What keeps some other gliding body, low
Under the moon or high above the sun,
From interrupting the bright shower of light?
Or, if her brightnesses are all her own,

Why can't she tire, at some fixed period,
While passing through the airs that murder light?

To sum it up: I have, by now, made clear
How through the azure areas of sky
Things happen, so that we may come to know
The various courses of the sun and moon,
What force, what cause, impels them, how their light
May darken unsuspecting areas,
Flicker, and flash, and flood the world again
With bright illumination. Now I turn
To our own earth's beginnings, to how the fields
All gently made decision what new birth
To send to the shores of light, or to commit
To the whims of the wind.

                              In the beginning, earth
Covered the hills and all the plains with green,
And flowering meadows shone in that rich color;
Then into air the various kinds of trees
Luxuriant in rivalry arose,
And just as feathers, hair and bristles grow
First on the bodies of all beasts and birds
So the new earth began with grass and brush,
And then produced the mortal animals
Many and various. Creatures such as these
Could not have fallen from the sky, nor come
Out of the salt lagoons. They are earthborn,
And truly earth deserves her title *Mother*,
Since all things are created out of earth.
Even today creatures arisen from earth
Are shaped by rain and by the warmth of sun;
No wonder then that in the past when earth
And air were younger, more and larger things
Came into being, first the fowls of the air,
The various birds that break their shells in the spring
As locusts do in summer when they leave

Their crinkled husks in search of livelihood.
In that time past earth was indeed prolific,
With fields profuse in teeming warmth and wet,
And so, wherever a suitable place was given,
Wombs multiplied, held to the earth by roots,
And as each embryo matured and broke
From fluid-sac to air, nature would turn
In its direction pores or ducts of earth,
Channels from which a kind of milk-like juice
Would issue, as a woman's breasts are filled
With the sweet milk after her child is born.
Earth gave her children food, the atmosphere
Such clothing as they needed, and the grass
A soft rich bed; that new and early world
Held no harsh cold, no superfluity
Of heat, no storm of wind; such forces also
Were in their infancy.

               I repeat, the earth
Deserves the name of Mother; by herself
She made the race of men, and in their season
The breed of beasts, those mountain stravagers,
The birds of the air in all their variousness,
But since there has to be, at last, an end
Of parturition, earth has given up
Like a worn-out old woman; time does change
The nature of the whole wide world; one state
Develops from another; not one thing
Is like itself forever; all things move,
All things are nature's wanderers, whom she gives
No rest; ebb follows flow, disdain succeeds
On admiration. Time indeed does change
The nature of the whole wide world; one state
Of generation follows on another,
So earth no more has power to produce
What once she bore, but can give birth to things
Impossible before.

In those first days
Earth tried to make all kinds of monstrous freaks,
Men-women, creatures with no feet, no hands,
Dumb ones without a mouth, blind ones who had
No faces to look out of, some whose legs
And arms were so tight-wound around their torsos
They couldn't do a thing, go anywhere,
Dodge trouble, grab for anything they'd need—
And all this weird assortment earth produced
In vain, since nature would not let them grow.
They could not reach to any flourishing,
Find nourishment, be joined in acts of love.
Prerequisite, we know, are many things
Before a species can survive—it needs
Food first of all, and reproductive parts
Whereby the seeds of life can find their way
From male to female, and their bodies join
In mutual delight.

In those old days
Many attempts were failures; many a kind
Could not survive; whatever we see today
Enjoying the breath of life must from the first
Have found protection in its character,
Its cunning, its courage, or its quickness,
Like the fox, the lion, and the antelope.
And there are many animals we guard
With our protection, for their usefulness:
The watchdog, beasts of burden, woolly sheep,
Horned cattle, all those eager refugees
Who left the wilderness in search of peace
And provender they had not planned to earn
But which we gave them for their services.
But those to which nature made no such gift,
Neither their own innate capacity
For living nor their usefulness to us
For which, in turn, we'd give them food and safety—
Such creatures, in the shackles of their fate,

Lay easy victims of their predators
Till nature brought the species to extinction.

Centaurs there never were; nor could there be
At any time such double-natured freaks,
Twin-bodied, incompatibly combined,
Their forces all uneven, thisway-thatway.
Even thick wits should know this for a fact.
In horses three-year-olds are near their prime;
Does this apply to humans? Some of them
Are hardly weaned by then. At twelve, a horse
Is old, worn out, and dying, but a boy
Just entering adolescence. Don't believe
That Centaurs are, or can be, constituted
From seed of men and horses; don't believe
In Scyllas, either, semi-mermaids, rigged
With sea-hound girdles. What monstrosities!
Their parts, we see, are in conflict with each other,
They do not flourish equally, grow old
At the same time; they share no mutual fire
For mating, keep no common usages,
Don't even enjoy the same delights. A goat
Battens on hemlock; what killed Socrates?
No tawny lion is immune to fire,
Neither is anything else if flesh and blood
Are in its make-up, so how could there be
Chimaeras, three in one, lion in front,
And snake behind, and in between the two
This fire-exhaling entity? Any one
Who figures animals like these were born
When and because the earth and sky were new
Depends too much on a pretty silly term—
Newness, forsooth! You'll find him pretty soon
Babbling more stuff like this, how rivers of gold
Ran over the earth, how emeralds hung from trees,
How men were born with such dynamic limbs
They'd prance through oceans, or, with a twist of the wrist,
Make sky revolve. In those first days when earth

Produced the animals, it is a fact
That earth held many, many kinds of seeds,
But that's no sign that herds could be created
In mixtures like cow-horses, or goat-pigs,
Especially since now, all over earth,
With all her great abundance, grains and grass
And trees that make us happy cannot blend
In complex fusion; each conforms in kind
To its own ritual, and all observe
The proper bounds decreed by nature's law.

The human race was tougher then: why not?
They were sons of a tough mother, and their bones
Were bigger and more solid, suitable
For stronger nerves and sinews, less distressed
By heat and cold, strange victuals, or disease.
For many centuries men led their lives
Like roving animals; no hardy soul
Steered the curved plowshare, no one understood
Planting or pruning. What the rain and sun
And earth supplied was gift enough for them.
Acorns were staple diet, or they fed
On arbute-berries, which we see today
Scarlet in wintertime—but long ago
There were more of them, much bigger, and the earth
Out of her blooming newness offered much—
No fancy fare, but adequate. The streams,
The springs, called men to quench their thirst, as now
Bright cataracts thundering over mountain-falls
Summon the thirsty and far-ranging beasts.
Then in their wanderings men came to know
The sanctuary areas which the nymphs
Considered home, where over the smooth stones
Water would ripple, brim above green moss
To even smoothness. People did not know,
In those days, how to work with fire, to use
The skins of animals for clothes; they lived
In groves and woods, and mountain-caves; they hid

Under the bushes when a sudden storm
Of wind or rain assailed their shagginess.
They had no vision of a common good,
No common law nor custom. What each man
Was given by Fortune, that he carried off,
Or, it may be, endured. He taught himself
To live and to be strong. And Venus joined
The bodies of lovers in the woods; a girl
Shared a man's appetite, or perhaps succumbed
To his insistent force, or took a bribe:
Acorns, or arbute-berries, or choice pears.

Relying on their strength and speed, they'd hunt
The forest animals by throwing rocks
Or wielding clubs—there were many to bring down,
A few to hide from. When the nighttime came,
They'd lump their shaggy bodies on the ground,
Much like wild boars, under a coverlet
Of leaves or brush, and when the sun went down
They did not try to trail him across the fields
With loud lament and panic. They lay still,
Buried in slumber, patient, till the sun
Raised his red torch above the world again,
For from their earliest childhood, they had seen
Light alternate with darkness; this they took
For granted, with no wondering, no dread
Lest night hold earth in everlasting thrall
With sunlight gone. What made them much more anxious
Was that wild animals would often make
Their sleep a fatal risk; if they caught sight
Of a lion or wild boar, they'd leave their homes,
Their rocky caves, and in the dead of night
Concede their leafy beds to their savage guests.
Mortality was not much greater then
Than now in our time; individuals
Were caught and eaten by wild animals,
And moaned and groaned and filled the woods with woe
Seeing themselves entombed in living flesh;

And even those who managed to escape
With bodies gnawed and chewed on, pressed their hands
Over their pustulent sores, invoking Hell
With dreadful cries, until their agony
Ended in death—they had no way of aid,
No knowledge of the treatment of a wound.

But no one day slew thousands on the field
Of battle, nor did ocean surges sweep
Shipping and men on rocks. In vain the sea
Rose, raged and stormed, or put aside his threats
Offering false deceptive calm. No man
Was fooled, for no man was a mariner,
Nobody knew the evil art of sailing.
It was lack of food that killed men in the past;
Today it's over-indulgence and excess.
They often, in their ignorance, killed themselves
By accident with poison. We are wiser,
We dose, or treat, our patients. Or our victims.

Next, with the use of fire and huts, and hides
Or furs for clothing, when a woman stayed
Joined to one man in something like a marriage,
With offspring recognized, that was the time
When first the human race began to soften.
Fire kept their bodies from enduring cold,
Lust sapped their energies, and children broke
Their parents' haughty spirit by their wheedling,
And even neighbors started forming pacts
Of nonaggression: *Do not hurt me, please,*
And I'll not hurt you, were the terms they stammered.
Men asked protection for their little ones
As well as for their wives; with voice and gesture
They made it clear that there was nothing wrong
In pitying the weak. They did not quite
Establish universal harmony,
But some of them came reasonably close—

Enough, at least, to keep the race alive
And propagating.

Nature drove them on
To use their tongues for speech, and they contrived,
For their convenience, names for things. Just so,
Children, before they learn to manage talk,
Point little fingers to distinguish objects.
All creatures sense their own potential ways—
An angry calf whose horns are not yet knobs
Will try to butt and shove, and lion cubs
Or panther kittens fight with teeth and claws
Even when the teeth are milk teeth, and the talons
Soft patty-paws; nestlings of every kind
Trust their uncertain wings in skittery flight.

Now don't suppose one single person gave
The names to things, and then taught other men the words.
That's nonsense. Why should such a fellow have
The power to distinguish things with names
While all the rest, it seems, just could not do it?
Besides, if others had not somehow managed
To use their voices to communicate
Where would foreknowledge of such useful art
Have risen from? Where would one man alone
Gain power to know, or anyway imagine,
What he proposed to do? All by himself
He could not force them, make them by the hundreds
Willing to learn the names of things; the deaf
Are hard to reach by knowledge or persuasion,
They would not let this idiotic racket
Be dinned into their inexperienced ears.
It's much more probable that the human race
Collectively with active voice and tongue
Gave names to things, with varying response
To varied stimuli. Even the dumb beasts,
The inarticulate animals, make sounds

That indicate emotions, fear, or pain,
Or even happiness. This is obvious.
Bloodhounds, when you annoy them, start by growling
Inside their jowls, or bare their teeth and snarl,
Crescendo to the loud full-throated bark.
Again, the sounds are different when they nuzzle
Their puppies, paw them around in play, pretend
To nip, or gobble them up, from when they howl
In some deserted house, or slink away
In terror of a whipping. Is there not
A difference in the whinny of a stallion
Loose with the mares, from when he snorts a challenge
To other studs, or makes a nickering sound
Just for the hell of it? Birds also wheel,
The hawks, the gulls, the ospreys, calling loud,
Skimming the waves in search of food, but giving
A different cry when they must fight to keep
Their prey from other birds. And weather, too,
Can make a difference—ravens and crows
Are not the same when prophesying rain
As when they summon wind. If animals,
Dumb beasts, can utter such dissimilar sounds
For different feelings, mortal man must be
At least as able by his voice to mark
Distinctions between objects.

                    Silently
You may be asking questions about fire.
Lightning first brought it down to men on earth
And every flame comes from that origin.
We notice many things glow hot when struck
With flames from heaven, but we've also seen
Boughs rub each other on a windy day
Till sparks, or even sheets of flame emerge
Out of that friction. Mankind's gift of fire
May well have started either way. The sun
Later showed people how to cook their food,
To soften it by heat, since they observed

Many a thing untoughened when his rays
Were warm across the fields.

              So day-by-day,
They changed their former ways of living, taught
By men of lively wit and kind intent.
Kings started founding cities, building walls
Around the heights for refuge and defense.
They made division of the herds and lands
According to men's qualities, their strength,
Their wit, their beauty—virtues highly prized
In those old days; but later on, with wealth
And the discovery of gold, the strong,
The beautiful, all too easily forsook
The path of honor, more than willingly
Chasing along behind the rich man's train.
Whereas, if man would regulate his life
With proper wisdom, he would know that wealth,
The greatest wealth, is living modestly,
Serene, content with little. There's enough
Of this possession always. But men craved
Power and fame, that their fortunes might stand
On firm foundations, so they might enjoy
The rich man's blessèd life. What vanity!
To struggle toward the top, toward honor's height
They made the way a foul and deadly road,
And when they reached the summit, down they came
Like thunderbolts, for Envy strikes men down
Like thunderbolts, into most loathsome Hell,
For Envy always blasts exalted things
Above the level of the commonplace.
So it would be a better thing by far
To serve than rule; let others sweat themselves
Into exhaustion, jamming that defile
They call ambition, since their wisdom comes
Always from other mouths, and all their trust
Is put in hearsay; when do they believe
Their own good sense and feelings? Never, never.

As it was in the beginning, so it is
Now, and forever shall be.

                So the kings
Got theirs, and majesty came tumbling down,
Sceptres and thrones in dust, and diadems
Bloodstained, mob-trampled, wailing, honor lost.
What was once-too-much-feared becomes in time
The what-we-love-to-stomp-on. So it goes
From heights of power to scum and dregs, from rule
To anarchy, and every man for himself
Till finally they grow sensible enough
To establish courts of law, and even use them,
Sick of their feuds and weary to exhaustion
Of violence piled on violence, where each man,
If he is judge, exacts in vengeance more
Than any decent law would ever inflict.
So men, being utterly tired of violence,
Are willing enough to suffer and submit
To legal codes. The fear of punishment
Does moderate our quest of life's rewards;
Evil and force and fraud are snares around
Their perpetrators; men who rise descend,
Return to where they started from; it's hard
For a disturber of the common peace
To live his life in calm serenity.
Even though he fools the race of men and gods,
He'd better not believe this state of things
Will always be a secret; many men
Talk in their sleep, or in delirium raving
Inform against themselves, broadcast a list
Of crimes too long concealed.

                Now comes the task,
By no means difficult, to say what cause
Proclaimed, across great nations, the rule of gods
And filled the towns with altars, and took care
To establish solemn rites and festivals

Which even in our great pomp and circumstance
Flourish, are held in reverence, in awe—
So much so that the whole wide world keeps on
Rearing new shrines to throng on holy days.
In that time long ago, men wide awake
Saw the distinguished presences of gods
With glorious appearance; and in sleep
Beheld their beauty even more magnified;
And so, to these, men granted sentience
Because they seemed to move their limbs, to speak
Proud language, consonant with their mighty power,
Their shining beauty. They must be, men thought,
Immortal, since they never seemed to change,
And with such potency as theirs no force
Could do them damage, and their fortunes were
Supremely blessèd, with no fear of death.
In dreams men saw them working miracles
Yet never tiring; and men's wonderment
Watched how the season's variable rounds
Followed an order they could not discern,
So they evasively assumed the gods
Must be responsible, and all things went
At their caprice. They gave them homes in heaven
Since that was where night and the moon and the sun,
The moon and day and night and night's austere
Signals, night-wandering torches of the sky,
Clouds, sun, rain, snow, winds, thunderbolts, and hail,
The abrupt blast, the low long-drawn-out rumbling,
All had their residence.

                    What sorry creatures!
Unhappy race of men, to grant the gods
Such feats, and add bitter vindictiveness.
What sighs and groans they gave themselves, what wounds
For us today, what tears for our descendants!
Is this devotion—putting on a veil,
Making yourself all too conspicuous
Turning in the direction of a stone,

Running to all the altars, falling flat,
Prone on the ground, holding out hands to pray,
Sprinkling the altars with the blood of beasts,
Swine, sheep, and ox, entwining vow with vow?
Ah, no. In true devotion lies the power
To look at all things with a peaceful mind.
Otherwise, contemplating that great world
Of heavenly space bejewelled with the stars
And pondering the ways of sun and moon,
We find our hearts, obsessed by evils, take
A new anxiety: must we face the power
Of gods almighty, who can make the stars
Revolve in all their brightness? Lack of sense,
Reason impoverished, harry the mind with doubt
Whether the world once had an origin
And whether it may also have an end,
A limit, when the ramparts of the world
Break down from all the stresses and the strains,
Or whether, by provision of the gods,
They have eternal safety, and are borne
Forever through the easy sweep of time
Scorning the eons' mighty violence.
Whose mind does not contract in panic fear
Of gods? Whose knees don't shake and knock together
When the earth shudders at a lightning blast
And thunder's rumble rolls along the sky?
Don't peoples tremble, haughty monarchs cower
Supposing that the hour of doom has come
For some base action, for some arrogant word?
When a wild hurricane sweeps an admiral
With his ships, his legions, and his elephants
Across the seas, does he not turn to prayer,
Approach the gods with vows, a trembling wretch
Imploring peaceful breezes, favoring airs?
And all in vain—the whirlwind bears him down
To the rocky shoals of death. How true it is
Some hidden force grinds down humanity,
Tramples its power-symbols in the dust,

Treats rod and axe with ridicule and scorn.
So when the whole world trembles under us
And shaken cities fall, and doubts assail,
What wonder if our generations know
Self-loathing, and most willingly concede
All glory, laud and honor to the gods
Who govern everything?

                   Our topic now
Is the discovery of metal, bronze,
Gold, iron, silver, lead—all this occurred
From the great heat of mountain forest-fires
Which lightning set, or savages at war
Employed to terrify their enemies;
Or possibly the opulence of the earth
Led men to clear its wealth, convert the woods
To open harvest-fields, kill the wild beasts,
Enrich themselves with spoil, for pits and fires
Were weapons of the hunt before the days
Of nets and coursing hounds. Well, anyway,
Wherever fire went crackling through the woods
In devastating racket, and the crust
Of earth was baked to a crisp, from underground
Through the hot veins into dry basins oozed
A flow of gold or silver, bronze or lead,
And when men, later, saw this gleam and shine
After its hardening, *What lovely stuff!*
They thought, and took it in their hands, and found
It kept the shape of the mold it once had filled.
So, they concluded, nuggets such as these
Were pliant, might be given any shape,
Be honed to the finest edge, for arms of war
Or tools of peace, the sword-blade, axe, or plane,
The chisel, hammer, awl. They tried at first
To make such instruments from gold or silver
Rather than bronze or copper, but they learned
The precious metals were too pliable,
So bronze had greater value in those times

Than gold, whose useless edge was blunt and dull.
How different now! The whirligig of time
Effects its changes—worth to worthlessness,
Meanness to splendor, honor to disdain.
You hardly need me, Memmius, at this point.
Surely you have the wit to figure out,
All by yourself, how men discovered iron.
They fought at first with hands and nails and teeth,
Stones, branches, and (a little later) fire,
And then they learned the use of iron and bronze—
Actually bronze came first, more flexible
And there was much more of it. Men used bronze
To plough the earth, to furrow waves of war,
To plant the seeds of wounds, expropriate
Cattle and pasture; every naked thing
Surrenders easily to men in arms;
So, little by little, iron's tougher edge
Took precedence, made the bronze sickle cheap.
When everybody has an iron sword,
The odds again are even.

                    In their wars
Men fought on horseback first, and plied the reins
Keeping the right hand free to whirl the sword,
Before they risked the chariot yoke and wheels.
Two horses were enough at first, then four
Were harnessed, and the car was big enough
To carry drivers, scythes, and fighting men.
Next thing we saw were those Lucanian herds
With towers on their backs, the horrible
Snake-snouts they used for hands; our enemies,
The Carthaginians, taught them to endure
The wounds of war, to trample Mars, his hosts
Into confusion's mob. The gloom of War
Is a great breeder of the horrible,
Heavier, day by day, the womb of dread.

Men put their bulls to services of war,
Turned wild boars loose against their enemies,

Or used, for shock troops, lions, with a corps
Of special trainers, armed and tough, to see
They never went too far. What foolishness!
The lions, hot with slaughter, took no heed
Whose ranks they broke; they tossed their manes, ran wild,
Stampeded cavalry; worse than the males,
The females hurled their bodies in great leaps
At any who dared face them, jumped on the backs
Of those who ran or stood there unsuspecting.
It was not enough to hurt men, knock them down,
They wound themselves around their victims, dug
With tooth and claws, in fierce embrace. The bulls
Would toss and trample no matter whom, would gore
And disembowel the horses, then paw the ground
As if in further threat. The wild boars dyed
Their white tusks red, they dyed with red the spears
Left in their bodies; horse and foot alike
Went down before them. Horses tried to swerve
Or rear and paw the air, much good that did them—
You could see them hamstrung, sprawling, heavily fallen—
If you'd ever thought them tame domestic herds
In the old days at home, you'd change your mind
Seeing them now, all hot in action, fired
By wounds, noise, flight, stampede, confusion, terror,
Beyond recall; and every kind of beast
Reverting to the wild, as elephants
Cruelly hurt will do today—attack,
Inflict on their own camp wounds like their own,
Then scatter. Could all this be true? I wonder.
It seems almost impossible for men
Not to have had the least presentiment
Of common doom let loose on all mankind.
Still, you might argue that not only here
On this our earth is folly such as this
Peculiar to the nations, but routine
With folk of whatsoever habitat.
Creatures far out in space no doubt behave
As we do, not desiring victory—
Oh no, of course not!—but to give the foe

A taste of sorrow. Populations die
If they disarm (as everybody knows).

For clothes, men tied things on, any old way
At first; the textile arts developed later
After the age of iron and its use
In fashioning treadles, heddles, spindles, looms
And all such clattering apparatus. Men
Are better at these arts than women are,
Much more ingenious, cleverer, but somehow
Farmers, who pride themselves on being tough,
Got the idea that this was fancywork,
So left it to the women.

                    Mother Nature
First gave us demonstrations of the way
Sowing might operate; the acorns fell
Under the oaks, bushes (or birds) dropped berries
Whose seeds in time became small shoots, a swarm
New risen, and men learned the stranger craft
Of grafting, or of planting slips in the earth,
Tried cultivation of their little plots,
Found methods of improving wilder growth
By patience and by gentleness, the way
Trainers succeed in taming other stock.
They made the woods climb higher up the mountains
Yielding the lowlands to be tilled and tended—
With meadow, pool, and stream, with oats and wheat
On the low plains—and higher on the hills
Vineyards to make men glad, and olive trees
Whose gray-green color marked the boundary
Up hill, down dale, so you could see all things
Charming, and all things different, all adorned—
Sweet orchards, lovely hedgerows.

                         As for music,
Men started first by imitating birdsong.
That came before they made up little tunes

With words to please the ear; and the stir of a breeze
Through reedy hollows whispering conveyed
Hints of the Pan-pipe. Pretty soon they tried
The sweet but sadder melodies they could make
With fingers on the flute, the native reed
Found in the pathless woods or upland groves
Where shepherds dwell, almost in idleness,
Almost in solitude, with music's charm
After a good square meal (for that's the time
Music gives most delight) to ease the spirit.
Often they sprawled on the soft meadow grass
Beside a stream, under a lofty tree,
And things went well at very little cost,
Especially when the season smiled, and spring
Stippled the greenery with colored flowers.
Then there were jokes, good talk, and laughter; then
The rustic Muse was at her liveliest
And fun and foolishness bade people twine
Wreaths around heads and shoulders, and step out
Stiff-legged, *hayfoot, strawfoot!* in a march
Or maybe it was a dance—it made them laugh,
Titter and giggle at this brave new world
So strange and wonderful. Who needed sleep
When they could blend their voices in the song
Or curve the lip around the reed-pipes' tops?
Even today men who must keep awake
Continue this tradition; they have learned
A stricter sense of time, but even so
I doubt they have more joy in song and dance
Than those old woodland aborigines.
We make the most of what's available
And love it dearly at first (unless we've known
Something much happier), then by-and-by,
Discover some improvement, change our taste
For old-time satisfactions. So men lost
Their appetite for acorns, left their beds
Of leaves and hay, despised the furry garb
They used to wear, such finery of style

That he who had first affected it aroused
Envy enough to cost him death by ambush,
His murderers tearing the prize apart,
All bloody, and no use to anybody.
Skins then, and cloth of gold and purple now
To give men's lives anxieties and wars;
And we're the worse, for in the ancient days
Cold was a cruel torture if a man
Had nothing he could wrap around himself.
But we're not hurt a bit by lack of gold
And purple and brocade; a poor man's cloak
Will keep us just as warm. The human race
Forever toils in vain, forever wastes
Time over empty worries, never knows
The limits of possessiveness, the brief
Capacity of pleasure for increase.
So, ever so slowly, we have brought our lives
To the great tidal depths of storm and war.

The watchmen of the world, the sun and moon,
Traversing heaven's revolving areas
Taught men about the season's annual round,
The fixity and order of the scheme.
By now men spent their days hedged all about
By battlements; they cultivated land
Marked off by boundaries; seas were a bloom
Of sailing vessels; friends and allies made
Pacts of agreement; and the bards began
To celebrate high deeds; but alphabets
Had not been long in use, and so our time
Cannot rely on letters for accounts
Of earlier history, but must depend
On reason's searching industry and power.
Ships, farms, walls, laws, arms, roads, and all the rest,
Rewards and pleasures, all life's luxuries,
Painting, and song, and sculpture—these were taught
Slowly, a very little at a time,
By practice and by trial, as the mind

Went forward searching. Time brings everything
Little by little to the shores of light
By grace of art and reason, till we see
All things illuminate each other's rise
Up to the pinnacles of loftiness.

Book VI

Athens of bright renown was first to bring
The gift of grain to troubled humankind,
Gave new vitality, established laws,
And first made life more than endurable;
She blessed in the sweetness of her boon a man
Who told the truth completely, so endowed
That now beyond his death his glory seems
Almost divine, exalted to the stars.
For when he saw that mortals on this earth
Had all or nearly all that need requires,
Security almost complete, were rich,
Were powerful, were honored, and were proud
Of their sons' recognition and renown,
And yet at home each had an anxious heart—
Life was one long vexation, never a pause,
No let-up in the daily cries of rage,
Of passionate complaining. So there must,
He knew, be some corruption in the jar,
The vase, the vessel of life—enough to spoil
Whatever good came through it from without.
Either it leaked, impossible to fill,
Or stank and fouled its contents. So he cleansed
Our hearts by words of truth; he put an end
To greeds and fears; he showed the highest good
Toward which we all are aiming, showed the way,
A straight and narrow path; he taught, besides,
What evils every here and there confront
The lives of men; how this is natural
As well as manifold, and may occur
By chance or violent intent, in line

With nature's preparations; but her drives,
Her onslaughts, can be baffled, once we learn
The proper sally ports to counter from.
He proved that it was mostly vain and wrong
For human hearts to suffer tides of troubles,
Inflict anxiety upon themselves;
And just as children, fearing everything,
Tremble in darkness, we, in the full light,
Fear things that really are not one bit more awful
Than what poor babies shudder at in darkness,
The horrors they imagine to be coming.
Our terrors and our darknesses of mind
Must be dispelled, then, not by sunshine's rays
But by insight into nature and a scheme
Of systematic study. Let me, then,
Still weave the texture of my argument.

I have shown that all the reaches of the world
Are mortal, that the heavens are born, and die;
I have shown most things that happen there, and must:
There is more to learn. Ride lofty with me now
Into the gales; behold how the winds' anger,
Once they are gentled, turns all things to peace.
Well, so it is with other things men see
In heaven, on earth, and tremble in suspense,
Debase their minds in terror of the gods,
Grovel because compulsive ignorance
Proclaims divine authority and sway.
Students, even those who have learned the lesson well
That gods lead lives supremely free of care,
May wonder, now and then, by what intent
This thing or that can happen, most of all
In areas overhead. This wonderment
Leads to confusion, leads them to regress
To obsolete religious awe, to invoke
A bitter lordship for themselves, poor fools—
Believers in almighty gods, and blind,
Credulous, ignorant of what can be

And what cannot, limits and boundaries,
Systems determined and immutable—
And so they wander, borne along in blind
Unreason. Spit out all such stuff, I tell you,
Stop having thoughts unworthy of the gods,
Alien to their serenity. Affront
To their high holiness can do you harm—
Not that their lofty power can be so hurt
That it would thirst for vengeance in a rage
For retribution—but that you yourself
Will feel convinced that mighty tidal waves,
Huge seas of anger, roll, and flood, and break
Against your littleness, while all the while
They have not even noticed, and their calm
Is quite unbroken. But you cannot go
Serenely toward their altars; you are blind
To the benignant holy images
They send as heralds of divinity;
And what your life may be in consequence
Perhaps you realize. I have tried, you know,
To ward this off, to use true reasoning
Against the danger, spoken many words,
But have not finished, still must give my lines
The ornament of polished verse. We must
Consider the scheme and aspect of the sky,
Must sing of storms and the bright lightning flash,
Their acts, the reasons for them. Any fool
Can chart the sky into sixteenths and scare himself
To see fire flash from Area This-or-that,
Zigzag through Somewhere-else, or penetrate
The impregnable and issue out again.
An ignoramus never understands
What causes things like these, and so he thinks
The gods must be responsible.

                         Ah, Muse,
Subtle Calliope, repose of men,
Delight of gods, lead me as on I run

Toward the last white chalk-line, be my guide
Till I am given the final crown of praise.

To start with: the blue skies are thunder-shaken
Because high-flying clouds collide and clash
When the winds fight each other. A calm sky
Means quietude, but when cloud masses form
Then all the more loud-rumbling sounds the thunder.
Clouds cannot be like stones or baulks of wood,
As thick as these in texture, nor as frail
As mist or flying smoke; if they were so,
They'd fall of their own heaviness like stones,
Or be like smoke, unable to contain
Chill snow and rain of sleet. The noise they make
Sounds over the levels of the world outspread
The way a theatre-awning snaps as it flaps
Between the poles and uprights, or in gusts
Rips with a crackle, like heavy paper torn,
Like sheets on clotheslines when the wind is blowing;
And sometimes, too, it happens that the clouds
Do not collide head-on, but scrape each other
Along their sides, and drag with grate and rasp
Till they haul free. And there's another way
Whereby all things seem heavily thunder-shaken
And the great ramparts of the universe
Suddenly leap apart when the wind's force
Whirls into the core of cloud, and there shut in
Bores out a hollow center with a crust
Of cloud around it; later, when this wind
Smashes the shell, then the torn cloud explodes
With terrifying crash. A child's balloon
Or a bladder full of air pops the same way
With sound all disproportionate to its size.

Then too the clouds make noises when the winds
Go blowing through them as a hurricane
Sweeps through a forest; clouds resemble trees,
As we have often noticed, in their branching,

Their general rough-and-raggedness. They rustle,
Rattle, and creak, as leaves and branches do
With the northwesters tearing them apart,
And sometimes wind can take a cloud head-on
And shatter it, as here on earth below,
Though with less violence, we have seen its force
Uproot tall trees. Also among the clouds
Are combers whose low murmur as they break
Swells to a louder roar, the sound of surf
Along deep rivers or great seas. Sometimes
The force of lightning rips from cloud to cloud
So that its fire meets moisture; then it seethes,
Hisses, as long as white-hot iron does
When dipped in the vat. But the receiving cloud
May be the drier of the two, and then
We hear a long-continued crackling sound
Like forest fire wind-driven through the growth
Of laurel bushes. Nothing burns more loud
Than does Apollo's laurel. Finally,
The rattle of ice, the fall of hail, can cause
Sound, under the pressure of the winds that break
These mountainous dark sacks of sleet and snow.

It lightens, also, when the clouds collide
And send off particles or seeds of fire
Like stone, or steel on stone. So leaps the light
In the bright shower of sparks. The reason why
We hear the thunder after we see the flash
Is that sound travels with less speed than light.
By way of illustration—if you see
Far off a woodsman cutting down an oak
You'll see the axe-flash long before you hear
The sound of the chop—and so we see the lightning
Before we hear the thunder, though they both
Were born in the same fashion.

                              In this way
Clouds with swift light dye areas of air,
And storm-gleams shimmer. Wind, invading cloud,

Revolving (this I've said before), bores out
The center, thickens the surrounding crust,
Is heated by its own velocity
To melting point, the way a lump of lead
Sent from a sling dissolves across the air;
So, when the hot wind cuts the dark cloud through,
Its force, its pressure, sends out seeds of fire
That blink and dazzle our eyes before the sound
Of thunder strikes our ears. It's safe to say
This happens also when thick-massing clouds
Are piled above each other. From below
It is easier to see how wide they are
Than estimate the heights to which they rise.
But look—and you will see these mountain clouds
Swept by the winds across opposing air,
Or see them, over actual mountains piled
Above each other, wedging each other down,
Calm and at rest when the winds are buried deep.
Then you can learn how great their massiveness,
Their caverns under (so it seems) the jut
Of overhanging rocks; and these the winds
Fill when the storms arise, and roar in rage
Against confinement in the hollow clouds
Like animals in cages; back and forth
They prowl, they howl with angry noise, they seek
How to get out, they stir the seeds of fire
To blasts within the furnaces of cloud
Till they escape, all flashing.

                              This is why
The color of that quick-descending stream
Is gold—the clouds contain gold particles,
The seeds of fire; they must—when they are free
Of moisture we can see them flame and shine,
Absorb the glints of sunlight, redden, glow,
Condense, till the wind's pressure shatters them
Precipitate in fire-colored flash and flame.
It lightens also in a different way
When clouds are thinned by less ungentle airs

To gradual dispersal; and the fire
Comes down in easier fall, no nasty shock,
No tumult and no terror, hardly a sound.

What is the nature of thunderbolts? We find
Our answer in the marks they leave, the signs
Of heat burnt in, the reek of sulphurous air.
These are proofs of fire, not wind or rain. Besides,
They set roofs blazing in no time at all,
Lord it through all the rooms. Insidious
This fire was made by nature, and refined
More than all other fires, with particles
Diminutive, quick, and irresistible,
For lightning bolts go through the walls of houses
As voices do, or noise; they go through rocks,
Through bronze, they can fuse bronze and gold together
In a split second; wine evaporates
Under their force from bowls or jars which show
Never a crack; and this occurs because
The heat is so intense it opens up
All of the pores, and, boiling through, it melts
The motes of wine, dissolving them in ways
The sun could not accomplish in a lifetime,
So burning is this force, this flash, this fire,
So much more mobile, more majestical.

How thunderbolts are made, with striking power
Able to shatter towers, blow open walls,
Wrench beams and rafters, wreck and topple over
Heroic monuments, kill off beasts and men,
I'll now explain—why should I put you off
With promises? Don't be impatient. Listen!
Thunderbolts must be sent from clouds piled high
And very thick, for when the sky is clear
Or lightly overcast they never strike.
The evidence is obvious: when a storm
Begins to link chain lightning, that's the time
Clouds thicken all through air, and we suppose

All the dark gloom, forsaking Acheron,
Has filled the mighty hollows of the sky
To loom above us, black and terrible,
In a foul night of cloud. Or out at sea
A tower of black, a pillar of pitch, a flood
Compacted all of dark, comes pouring down
Heavy with whirlwind and with lightning bolt,
Distended so with its own fire and wind
That men on land in terror rush indoors.
All we can see is the base of a column of storm
Rising above us. Never would such black dark
Drown earth, unless cloud, massed and piled on cloud,
Rose high enough to take the sun away,
And never could such rain come pouring down
To swell the rivers and make ploughland swim
Were not the sky packed with excess of cloud
And every cloud so filled with wind and fire
That flash and rumble are continual.
Let me repeat—the hollow clouds contain
Infinite motes of heat; they must acquire
More from the rays of the sun; and when the wind
Herds them together—but even so drives out
A goodly number—it whirls among the pack
In such a way it whets the thunderbolt
By the hot friction in the double rage
Of its own speed, or contact with the fire;
So when violence of the wind grows hot
And the fire's impulse penetrates, the bolt
Is ripe, rips through the cloud and rides the air,
Lightens all places with its flash and flame,
With loud crash following; and the sudden burst
Shocks areas of sky, and tremors make
Earth shudder and the rumbling echoes roll
Skyward again, as storm and shock pervade
All areas of sense. The rain pours down
Heavy, profuse, the sky itself is flood,
Is fall of fire, is cataract of sound.
Sometimes, again, the violence of wind

Hits from without on clouds already hot
With a ripe thunderbolt, so fire erupts
At once in any direction as the blast
May make it go. And sometimes, also, wind
Starts with no blaze at all, but catches fire
As it speeds onward, losing in its course
Large elements that cannot pass through air,
Scrapes bodies infinitesimal in size
From the same air, fire-particles—the way
A leaden bullet in its flight will lose
Its attributes of stiffness and of cold
And melt or burn in air. The force of wind
May even be cold, may be devoid of fire,
And yet cause fire just from the violence
Of impact, as we now and then observe
When cold steel strikes cold stone. It all depends
On timeliness; its own rush of energy
Converts the coldest of material,
Lukewarm to white-hot stuff, or chill to fire.

The speed and impact of the thunderbolt
Ensue because the violence in the cloud
Is concentrated, every bit of force
Taut for momentum, loosening, escape.
Then, when the cloud no longer can contain
The increase of this force, it is expelled
As missiles are from catapults. Being made
Of smooth and tiny elements which move
With little opposition, small enough
To penetrate the narrowest openings,
No wonder it flies swiftly. Furthermore,
All objects having weight by nature tend
Downward, but start them with a push or shove,
Their speed is doubled, their momentum gains,
Their impact is more shattering, their sweep
Is more extensive, all their violence
Increases in proportion as they move;
Distance accelerates their drive, the motes
Being urged from all directions on one course,

And (possibly) from the air a bolt in flight
Picks up some bodies which can spur it on.
There are some things a bolt can penetrate
And leave unharmed, intact, for fire can slide
Through openings as water does. A bolt
Can also smash and shatter if its motes
Fall on the places where the particles
Of objects meet and join, and bolts dissolve
Both bronze and gold quite readily, being made
Of elements diminutive and smooth,
Insinuatory and insidious
At severance, dispersal, liquidation.

Autumn is one season when the starry halls
Of heaven are shaken, like our world below,
And blossoming spring is such another time.
Not winter, though, when the fires fail, and wind
Blows cold, and clouds are meager and mean. Halfway
Between the winter and the summertime
We find, in combination, every cause
Of lightning and of thunder. Heat and cold
Mingle and clash, things are discordant, air
Seethes in a turbulence of thermal winds,
And all of this is needed for the clouds
To manufacture thunderbolts. Heat's head
Devour's cold's tail; there's spring for you, a time
Of warfare and confusion, bound to brawls.
The same in autumn, turned the other way,
Winter's raw vanguard chopping at the rear
Of summer's ragged veterans. Call such times
The foul rifts of the year, and do not be
Surprised if many and many a thunderbolt
Is then hurled loose, if skies are dark with storm,
If winds and rain are allies against fire
In wars of which no augur knows the end.

This, then, is how to see the fiery bolt,
Its nature, how it operates; no need
To finger pages of Etruscan scrolls

Seeking for evidence of what the gods
May or may not intend; no need to chart
The course it flies, or how it penetrates
Defences, dominates, escapes again,
What power it has to damage. If the gods,
Jupiter and the others, shake the skies
With dreadful uproar, heaving fire around
At each one's whim, why don't they ever make
Persons of criminal impulse, not averse
To evildoing, breathe out fire, exhale
Sulphur from riddled chests? *That ought to teach them!*
Why are the blameless and the innocent—
With nothing on their consciences—involved,
Wrapped in the fires of heaven, annihilated?
Why aim at lonely places, waste their time
Hurling at deserts? Are they practicing,
Just warming up, just getting loose? And why
Do they allow their father's weapon, Jove's,
To blunt its point on the earth? Why, for that matter,
Does he permit such nonsense, and not save
The weapon for his enemies? One thing more—
Why does he never, out of a clear sky,
Let fly the roar and flash? Does he have to wait,
Till clouds appear, and then sneak into them
For better regulation of his aim?
What sense is there in firing on the sea?
Has he some quarrel with waves and swimming plains?
And why, especially if he thinks we should
Beware of lightning, why not let it fly
Where we can watch? If, on the other hand,
He wants to catch us off our guard, what sense
Is there in making darkness, rumble, din
In one location, giving us a chance
To see and dodge? Does any one believe
He shoots north, south, east, west, and all at once?
Or doesn't this ever happen? But of course
It does—as raindrops fall on many lands
Almost as may thunderbolts come down.

To end this—why does Jupiter let fly
His missiles at the holy shrines of gods,
His own included, break their images
Made with such artistry, and take away
Their standing with his wounding violence?
Why does he aim most often at the heights?
Why do we see the traces of his fire
Most often on the summits of the mountains?
From the foregoing we can find a clue
To what the Greeks call *presters*, how they fall
Into the sea, a pillar or a column
Let down, or hurled, around which water seethes
And spirals under vast revolving winds—
And ships caught in that whirling turbulence
Are in great danger. This phenomenon
Occurs because the violent force of wind
Cannot break through the cloud, but weights it down
Into the sea, a pillar or a column
A little at a time, as if a fist
Or forearm's pressure shoved it under water
And held it so, until at last it burst
And the wind's violence made the water seethe,
For whirlwinds in descent revolve and bring
The satellite cloud attached, but once they dump
Its heaviness in the water, then the winds
Work themselves loose, rush out, and churn the sea
With a roar of sound. Sometimes the whirl of wind
Is wrapped in cloud, or scrapes off particles
Of cloud from air, and imitates on land
These so-called *presters*. Then we get a squall
Of terrible force; but this on land is rare
Because of natural barriers like the hills
And mountain ranges; it occurs more often
Across the open ocean's wide expanse.

Clouds mass together when in lofty air
Numerous flying bodies meet and join,
So shaggy-textured that they lock and cling

Although their hooks and fasteners are most
Diminutive indeed; still, they suffice,
And so we got small cloudlets; these, in turn,
Unite with others like themselves, increase
In size, are borne by winds until the time
When a wild storm arises. Mountain peaks
Nearest the sky smoke oftenest with the swirl
Of sulphur-colored clouds. These form, we know,
Before our eyes can see them, frail and thin,
As the winds herd them toward the mountaintops
Where they appear, more closely packed, and rise
Toward upper air. It's obvious enough,
As our own sense has taught us when we climb
The mountain trails, that heights are windy places.
We learn this also from a seaside stroll,
See clothes hung up to dry, how they absorb
A sticky dampness, as if many things
Were lifting little increments for cloud
Out of its kindred element, the salt
Of ocean water. Out of every stream,
And even out of land, we watch the mist,
The murk of fog arising—hardly more
Than breath blown upward, but it fills the sky
With darkness, little by little builds the cloud—
While from above the heat of star-bright air
Bears down upon it, draws the mass of dark
Below the clearer blue. And it can be
That from beyond the universe we know
Come particles to form the scudding clouds,
For (as I've taught you) we can never count
The number of atomic particles,
Their sum being infinite; I have also shown
With what superlative speed they move across
Immeasurable space. No wonder then
If, in a moment only, storms can mass
With such great clouds, and darkness veil the seas,
Since through all capillaries of the sky,

Through all the world's most infinitesimal pores
The elemental bodies come and go.

Now I'll explain how, in the lofty clouds,
The moisture gathers and falls to the earth as rain.
First let me say that out of everything
Numerous motes of water rise to the clouds
And there increase, as do the clouds themselves
With all their contents, growing as our bodies
Grow with their blood and plasma, sweat and lymph.
Clouds also soak up liquid from the deep
Like hanging woolly fleeces borne by the wind
High over stream or ocean. When the clouds
Are nearly running over, full to the brim
With water-seeds, they labor to discharge
Their moisture in two ways: the force of wind
May push them in such masses, close together,
That their compression and compactness cause
The rain to fall, from the sheer weight of cloud,
From dense adhesion. But then, also, winds
May thin the clouds, dissolve them, as it were,
And the sun's heat precipitate the rain
As fire melts wax. Rains are most violent
Under the double pressure of their weight
And wind's commotion; for the rain pours down
In more continual fall when cloud on cloud
Piles high, and mist is borne along with mist,
And many, many motes and water-seeds
Are everywhere—even the steaming earth
Discharging wetness. Finally the sun
Through the storm-darkness sends the rays of light
Shining against the cloud-spray, and we see
The glory of the rainbow.

                 Other things,
Cloud-born, cloud-grown, but different, such as snow,
Wind, hail, frost, sleet, the rigid force of ice,

That hardener of rivers, the great wall
That stays them in their courses, all of these,
All, all, are comprehensible enough
If for the answers to your *How?* and *Why?*
You keep in mind their basic properties.

What causes earthquakes? You should realize
That earth below, like earth above, must have
Plenty of windy caverns, plenty of lakes
And pools and rocks and cliffs, and many streams
Deep down, rolling with heavy violence
Great rocks, drowned boulder-stones. No matter where,
The law is: *things are like themselves*. And so
With things like these below her surface, earth
Trembles, by ruin shocked, when time brings down
Her subterranean caves. Whole mountains fall
And from that cataclysm trembling spreads
Immediate, everywhere. Is it not true
That carts, even light-loaded ones, can make
The houses tremble as they clatter over
The cobblestones? or a loose chunk of rock
Under the iron rims of the wheels can cause
Buildings to seem to start and jump a bit?
Also it sometimes happens that underground
A mountainous landslide, loosened by a shove
From time, comes roaring, rumbling, sliding down
Into more lakes than one, and the earth shudders
As any vessel does, when what it holds
Slops at the sides, refusing to be still.

When through the hollows underground the wind,
From one direction gathered, blasts full force
At the deep caverns, earth, inclining, leans
Obedient to that rushing violence,
And houses in that same direction lean,
Come tumbling down, or threaten to, and hang
Their loosened timbers over emptiness;
And men, although they see so great a mass

Of earth collapse or slither toward its doom
Still are afraid to trust their senses, doubt
That ruin's time will bring upon the world
The sentence of destruction. But the wind
May blow the other way, and so forestall
The menace—save for this, no power could halt
The march of things to doom and nothingness.
But since they do reverse direction, turn,
Increase momentum of their counterflow,
Retreat across the plain of their attack,
So earth more often seems about to fall
Than truly falling; devastation's threat
Is worse than the reality—the world
Leans over and springs back, the weight returns
From the periphery to the proper core
And this is why all buildings wobble most
On the top levels, less in the middle, less,
Very much less, at the base.

                         There's another cause
Of this vast kind of temblor, when the wind
Or a tremendous quantity of air
Comes from beyond the world, or may arise
(No matter) from its own internal depth,
Pours into hollow caverns, roaring through
Those mighty vaults, until its violence
Breaks out of bounds, splits the terrain, creates
Chasm or canyon. This occurred, we know,
In Syria at Sidon, and again
At Aegium in Greece, where the air's blast
And the earth's quaking shook the cities down.
And there are other instances, of towns
Collapsing into earth, or ocean-drowned
With many of their citizens. The air
Need not burst forth completely if its whirling
Is violent enough below the ground,
Dispersing through earth's many openings—
In an intensity of shuddering

Making earth tremble, as the freezing cold
Will make us shudder and shake, against our will;
And so men tremble in a double fear
Lest houses over their heads come tumbling down
Or caverns, opening under the ground, devour
The mass of ruin. People have the right
To think whatever they please of earth and heaven,
To tell themselves these rest forevermore
On sure foundations, but sometimes it seems
Beliefs like these are undermined more than once,
From more than one direction, and men dread
Lest earth be yanked from under their feet, drop down
Into the bottomless abyss, and all
The sum of things, betrayed, be taken over
In the anarchic ruin of the world.

Men wonder that the sea does not increase
In size, with so much water pouring down,
Such confluence of all the streams and rivers;
Then add the wandering rains, the sweep of storms,
All sprinkling and all dowsing elements
That moisten all the lands and seas; include
Submarine springs—yet all of this adds up
To hardly more than a drop in that vast deep
Of ocean's plenitude. No wonder, then,
The sea does not increase; and anyway
The sun's evaporating force is strong
Enough to shrink it somewhat; we have seen
Clothes, not too well wrung out, hung up to dry
In the sun's rays. Now there are many seas
Widespreading, and though the sun from every one
Takes only a little at a time, it all
Adds up to a tremendous diminution;
And winds that sweep across these surfaces
Can also dry the waters, as we've seen
Roads harden over night, and mud become
Dry-caked, with crossing cracks. And I have shown
That clouds lift water from the ocean's plain

To sprinkle all the world, now here, now there,
When the rain falls or winds bring darkening.
Finally, since a porous quality
Inheres in earth, wherever it meets the sea,
Wherever the boundaries join, as water comes
From earth to sea, as counterflow seeps back
Out of salt ooze, it loses brackishness,
Is filtered and distilled, and makes its way
Once more, all sweet and fresh, in rivulets,
Channels and streams, to its appointed course.

The next thing to explain is how the fires
Burst with such violence through Etna's gorge.
That was no ordinary, commonplace,
Or middling kind of ruin, when the fire
Arose and fell on the Sicilian plain
Lording it so that all the neighbor lands
Turned their attention, seeing heaven bright
With flash, or dark with smoke, as all men's hearts
Were anxious: what subversive cosmic wreck
Could nature be contriving?

                 Things like this
Require your closest scrutiny; keep in mind
How vast, how infinite, the sum of things.
Our heaven is only the minutest part
Of the whole universe, a fractional speck—
Less than one individual compared
To the entirety of the earth. Remember—
Never forget this—once you see it plain
You will be rid of many puzzlements.
Are we one bit surprised if, when we know
We have a fever, the infection flames
Painfully through our muscles and our bones?
A foot swells gouty, or a toothache jumps,
Eyes water and blear as erysipelas
Seizes whatever it may and penetrates
Deep in the limbs. And why not, when there are

Seeds of sufficient evil in heaven and earth
To propagate disease unlimited,
With particles of pain unlimited,
Infinitesimal seeds, yet infinite?
In the same way, our heaven and our earth
Draw from the store of the vast universe
Enough of everything to shake our world,
To sweep our seas with whirlwinds, set such fires
Blazing from Etna that they seem to drown
The empyrean with flame; there can be floods
Of fire as well as water. "But this burning
Is out of all proportion!" So it seems—
The way some little creek he can jump across
Is like the father of waters to a man
Who never saw a river in his life.
The biggest man, the biggest tree in the world,
The biggest we can imagine, barely tops
The biggest we have seen. Yet everything,
Sky, sea, and earth—oceans, and lands, and skies—
Add up to nothing in the sum of things.
Enough digression! Let me tell you now
From what blast furnaces Mt. Etna's fires
Burst with such violence. That mountain mass
Is honeycombed with hollows, and it rests
On archways made of basalt. Air at rest
Is here, and wind in motion, and the wind
Involves the air in whirling, till they both
Are fast and furious, and the rocks are hot
Wherever they touch, and earth is hot, and fire
Borne on the wind shoots high, so high it bursts
Out of the mountain's crater. With it pour
Ashes and steam and darkness, smoke and rocks
Of weight beyond belief. Oh, never doubt
The force of this eruption! Furthermore,
Around the mountain's base the sea intrudes,
Withdraws again, leaving some elements
Like sand, or submarine rocks, or water-wind,

All sucked up toward the top, material
For those high mixingbowls (the word, in Greek,
Is *craters*). We just call them throats or jaws.

There are many things for which it's not enough
To specify one cause, although the fact
Is that there's only one. But just suppose
You saw a corpse somewhere, you'd better name
Every contingency—how could you say
Whether he died of cold, or of cold steel,
Of poison, or disease? The one thing sure
Is that he's dead. It seems to work this way
In many instances.

                    The summer Nile,
The only river in Egypt, floods the fields
In the warm season, possibly because
The Etesian winds, so-called, blow steadily
From northern areas, and retard the stream
At every delta, force its currents back
In all its channels. There is never a doubt
That winds like these, from the cold northern stars
Do blow against that river, which reverts
Toward southern climates where the men are black,
Where day is always noon. Or it may be
That a great heap of sand, piled up, blocks off
The rivermouths, when the sea, stirred by the wind,
Rolls the sand inward, so the river's course
Is more obstructed, less of a down-hill gliding.
Possibly, too, the rains are more profuse
Inland in summer, when the Etesian winds
Drive all the clouds southward and mass them there
Where the high mountains block their way, or squeeze them
Almost like sponges, or the melting snows
From Ethiopian heights, in summer sun,
Dissolve their whiteness over the plains below.

About Avernian regions and their lakes
A word of explanation. First of all,
The name comes from the Greek, *a-ornos*, birdless,
Because when birds fly over, they forget
The oarage of their wings, they slacken sail,
Fall headlong, limp-necked victims, onto earth
Or into water if a pool is there.
There's such a place near Cumae, with a reek
Of sulphur and the mist of steaming springs.
There's one inside the great Acropolis
In Athens, where Athena has her shrine.
Here raucous crows never come gliding down
Even when altars smoke with sacrifice.
The reason is not that they dread the spite
Of Pallas for their spying, as the bards
Of Greece have sung. By no means. But the place
Is pestilential, all by itself, its nature
Needing no help from goddesses. I've heard
Of such another spot in Syria
Where quadrupeds no sooner turn their steps
Than they come tumbling heavily down, like beasts
Slain for an offering to the gods below.
Effects like these derive from natural laws.
No need to fancy that the Gate of Hell
Yawns open here, or that the Gods Below
Are drawing people down to Acheron,
The Joyless Realm, the way that some folks think
Deer, by their breath, can get the snakes to move
Out of their holes. What rot! All I can do
Is try to state the simple truth.

I say,
As I have said before, there are on earth
All kinds of things, and some of them sustain
Our life, and some destroy it; furthermore,
Some things are suitable for the scheme of life
And others harmful; it would all depend
On what the creatures are—their variance

Is great, in essence, contour, texture, shape.
The ears let many things inimical
Pass through, and many noxious qualities
Pervade the nostrils; and the sense of touch
Must leave a lot alone, and eyes and tongue
Refuse maleficence in sight and taste.

Mankind has learned that many things oppress
Our nature, noisome things, or dangerous.
The shadows of some trees, for instance, fall
So heavily that headache seizes men
Who lie on the grass beneath; and Helicon
Produces, on its lofty heights, a tree
Whose blossom kills men by its nasty stench.
Such things as these come from the soil of earth
Which holds all kinds of particles, confused,
Then sorted out and passed along. A lamp
Snuffed out at bedtime leaves an after-smell
That stuns an epileptic; healthy men
Dislike it for a moment only. Women
Let fall their knitting and swoon if beaver-musk
Assails their senses at that time of the moon.
There are many other causes which effect
A lack of consciousness, or weaken spirit
Within the limbs. Take a hot bath too soon
After a hearty dinner—it won't be long
Before you find yourself loll off your throne,
Collapse into the water. Charcoal's reek
Can stupefy the brain unless you drink
Plenty of water as preservative.
The scent of wine can strike you like a blow
If you are feverish. Deep in the earth
Sulphur and pitch combine and stink, and miners
Probing the mother lode for silver and gold
Unearth aromas worse than any Skunktown.
That yellow metal breathes its hues on men,
It jaundices their faces, and they die
Too soon of occupational disease,

Compelled to spend their days in work like this.
Oh, yes indeed, earth pours out streams of death
Toward the vast readiness of atmosphere.

So as regards Avernus—there must be
Some noxious vapor rising there; and birds
As they encounter it unsensed, unseen,
Come plunging down this maelstrom of rank air;
And even after they fall they flutter and flop
Until the frenzy ends, and life's a vomit
Into the whirlpool of evil all around them.

Or—it's just possible—this towering force
Arising from Avernus, drives all air
So far away that there is only void
Or vacuum between the birds and earth
Where no wing possibly can ply its way,
Where every effort meets resistlessness,
So down they come through emptiness to doom.

Water is colder in wells in summertime
Since earth dries out in the heat and sends the motes
Of warmth more quickly upward, so, deep down,
The more the surface heat evaporates,
The colder is the moisture underground.
The opposite is also true: when earth,
Oppressed by cold, congeals and packs, it drives
Its residue of heat to the pools below.

At Ammon's shrine, or so men say, a spring
Is cold by day and hot at night, and this
Men marvel at too much and claim a sun
Below the ground must be responsible,
Making it boil when night has veiled the earth
In terrible black murk. This, I must say,
Is a long way from truth, for if the sun
Trying with all his might from dawn to dusk,
Could not so much as raise the temperature

More than a few degrees, even at high noon,
How could he, from beneath so thick a bulk
Of earth, bring water to a boil, with steam
Evaporating from it? But the sun
Has trouble enough, with all his fiery rage,
To make his heat pass through the walls of houses.
The explanation must be that the earth
Has more interstices around that spring
Than elsewhere in the world, and seeds of fire
Lie close to the water, so when earth rests dark
Under night's dewy shadow, it grows cold,
Contracts, as if a hand were squeezing it,
And squirts out all those orange-pips of fire
To warm the water. When the sun returns
To warm the world, to open its pores again,
The seeds of fire flow backward to their source,
The water's heat returns to earth, the spring
Is cold once more in the light of day. The sun,
Moreover, has a vibrant power of water,
Making it quiver, tremble, thin and part
So that what motes of fire it had are lost
In the same way that water itself can loosen
Its own intrinsic qualities of cold
And melt the bonds of ice.

                     There's a chill spring
Which kindles tow held over it: a torch
So lit continues burning, though it falls
Into the water, floats or swims with the wind.
There must be in such water many seeds
Of fire that rise through the whole pool, disperse
Exhaled to the air above; too few perhaps
To warm the water, but even so enough
To meet and join just over the surface, form
An unseen latent area of ignition.
Something like this occurs near Aradus
Where there's an ocean spring whose flow provides
Fresh water at its center, keeping back

The threatening circumference of brine;
And there are other springs where mariners
Happily find sweet water in ocean deeps.
In some such way the seeds of fire must break
Through water to ignite the tow. A wick,
If not too long extinguished, will break out
In flame before it meets the actual fire
Of the night-lamp you start to move it toward.
There are many other instances where fire
Can leap a gap, or seem to. That's enough
To explain that curious fountain at Dodona.

Next I'll discuss what laws of nature cause
Iron to be attracted by that stone
The Greeks call magnet. (They derive the name
From the Magnetes' country, where it's found.)
The stone men think is marvelous; it forms
A chain of downward links as many as five
Or even more suspended from each other,
Slightly swaying in the lightest breeze,
Yet never loosening hold, as if each one
Took from the medium of the one above
The power transmitted from the potent stone.

Such things as this require a basic course
In fundamentals, and a long approach
By various devious ways, so, all the more,
I need your full attention. Listen well.

In the first place, from everything we see
There is bound to be an everlasting flow.
Ah, look about you! Watch a glimmering pool
In the first shine of starlight, see the stars
Respond, that very instant, radiant
In water's universe. Does this not prove
How marvelous the swift descent from heaven?
Our other senses know of emanance
In fragrances, in sunlight's heat, in surge

Of surf-destroying sea walls, in the sound
Of voices calling always through the air,
In salt spray tasted as we walk the shore,
In bitterness imagined when our eyes
Watch someone pouring wormwood into water—
So from all things there is this constant flow,
This all-pervasive issue, no delay,
No interruption, and our sense responds
In recognition.

Let me repeat a lesson from Book I—
How porous all things are! This truth applies
In many instances, but most of all
In what I'm leading up to; once again
I hammer home this axiom: everything
Perceived by sense is matter mixed with void.
Rocks drip with moisture in caves, and sweat breaks out
All over our bodies. We grow beards, have hair—
Not only on our faces. All our food,
Distributed through the bloodstream, nourishes,
Brings growth to even our toe-nails. We can feel
Both cold and heat pass through a bowl of bronze
Or cups of gold and silver at banquet time.
And voices penetrate through walls of stone,
As odors trickle through, and heat and cold
And fire can force a passageway through iron.
Even the chain mail armament of sky
Is penetrable; through its chinks there come
Diseases from a world beyond, and storms
In earth or sky engendered make their way
To sky or earth, reciprocal; wherefore
We say once more, *How porous all things are!*

But not all bodies loosed from things possess
Identical impacts or effects. The sun
Bakes earth and dries it, but it melts the ice,
Thaws the high mountain snows, liquefies wax,
Makes molten streams of bronze or gold, but chars

Flesh, and will shrivel leather. Following fire,
Water will harden iron, but restore
Softness to skins and flesh. Wild olives are
(So bearded she-goats think) a treat as rare
As nectar and ambrosia, but men find
Nothing more bitter on any bush or tree.
Pigs run like mad from oil of marjoram
And fear all kinds of perfume; what we deem
Refreshing is to them a deadly bane.
But mud, which we consider worse than filth,
Is their ecstatic absolute delight,
They cannot get enough of wallowing in it.

Now one thing more, before I talk about
The theme I know I must: though porousness
Is an inherent quality of things,
Its nature varies; every object has
A nature of its own, its passageways
Different from the others. Living things
Have various kinds of sense perception; each
Receives, by its own medium, what it should.
Sound does not penetrate as odors do,
Nor sights insinuate themselves like flavors.
One thing, apparently, can trickle through rock,
Another seep through wood, another gold,
And still another emerge from glass or silver.
And some things move more swiftly than the rest
Along the selfsame ways. It follows, then,
The nature of the differing passageways
Brings this about with great variety
As we have shown before, since things possess
Great differences in the way their textures mesh.

So, with this preparation, what remains
Is easy enough. The mass of iron is drawn
Stoneward, because so many motes from stone
Are always flying outward, or some tide,

Some current, sweeps away the air that lies
Between the stone and iron. When this space
Is empty, then the motes of iron glide
Into the vacuum, meet and join, and so
The ring, complete, must follow. There is nothing
More tightly meshed in its first elements
Than iron is, that rough and chilly ore.
No wonder then that bodies drawn from this
Cannot, by very density, attain
A passage into void, without the ring
Following close behind—and this it does,
This is exactly what it does, it follows
Until it strikes the stone, and there it clings
In fastenings unseen. No matter where,
The process is the same; if we should have
An empty space, above, along, below,
Neighboring motes would rush in, all the time,
To fill it up, propelled by impulses
Beyond themselves. And there's the added fact
(To make things easier, another boost,
Another shove) that when the air is thinned
Before the ring, the space made emptier,
The air behind propels it from the rear
Such being its nature, circumambience
Forever buffeting. It pushes iron
When it can find a vacuum to enter
On one side or another; it will slip
Through many a crevice, most insinuous
Into the smallest particles, drive and thrust
As the wind drives a sailing vessel on.
All things must have within their substance air
Since things are never solid; and this air
Also surrounds and borders everything.
Therefore, since air is hidden deep in iron,
It knows commotion there, and from within
Assails the ring and moves it, to be sure,
Further along the course where it flung itself
In its initial impulse toward the void.

Sometimes the iron shrinks away from the stone,
A fickle fugitive or follower,
Now one thing, now another. I have seen
Filings of Samothracian iron dance
In frenzy in bronze bowls when magnet-stones
Were held beneath them. It would almost seem
As if they wanted nothing but escape
From the stone's presence. I suppose the bronze
Caused this antipathy, because its force
Entered the pores of iron first and left
No room for other entrants; so the stone,
Finding all channels in the iron blocked
And nowhere, as there used to be, a place
For motes of stone to swim, must beat and pound
The iron with its own current, or through bronze
Repel the element it would absorb
Without that barrier. Don't be surprised
That magnet-stones lack power on every ore,
For instance, gold, whose heavy weight resists
All penetration. Others are so light,
So widely meshed, the current flowing through
Meets no resistance, cannot drive them on.
Wood seems to be a substance of this kind,
While iron's nature lies between the two;
But given added particles of bronze
The magnet-stones repel it by their flow.
Such properties inhere in other things
As well. I could cite many instances
Of singular fusion: stones are held together
Only by mortar; wood needs glue—at times
When planks are fastened so, the grain of the board
Will crack and gape before the joints are loosed.
Wine can be mixed with water; tar cannot,
Nor olive oil—too heavy, or too light.
Your Tyrian crimson dye will blend with wool
So absolutely that no power on earth,
I should say ocean, ever could wash out
That stain incarnadine. Gold clings to gold

If one material and only one
Is used to effect the fusion. Tin alone
Can fasten bronze to bronze—but why go on
With instance after instance? Here's the point—
Some objects have reciprocal qualities,
One's fullness matching another's emptiness
Or *vice versa;* here it seems we get
The most ideal of fusions. There may be
Some combinations rather more loosely meshed,
Held, as it were, by links or hooks or rings
As with the iron and the magnet-stone.

Now I'll explain the causes of disease,
Whence plagues and pestilences rise to stun
Both man and beast with deadly virulence.
The seeds of many things, as I have shown,
Are necessary to support our lives.
By the same token, it is obvious
That all around us noxious particles
Are flying, motes of sickness and of death,
And when these gather, thickening the air,
The atmosphere is murderous with cloud
And murk descending; or, it may be, mist
Rises from earth, rotten with too much rain,
Too great excess of sun. Have we not seen
Travelers far from home who can't endure
The change of water or climate? Who believes
Britain and Egypt are alike? Who finds
Byzantium at Gibraltar? Are the Danes
Identical with Ethiopians?
In the four quarters of this varied world
Human complexions, human aspects, take
All sorts of different guise, and human ills,
Distresses, and diseases, also change
After their kind. Only in Africa
Is elephantiasis known; and gout prevails
In Attica more than elsewhere; the Achaeans
Are subject to infections of the eyes.

So different organs are susceptible
In different places, and the atmosphere
Is the controlling factor. When a sky
Hostile to us begins to move, or crawl,
Or glide, most serpent-wise, entwining all
With coils of cloud or mist, confusion stirs
Wherever it goes, and changes are enforced
In our familiar quarters, now corrupt,
Made kin to this new presence. So the plague
Falls on the water or the grain fields, falls
On other nourishment of beasts and men,
Or hangs suspended in the very air
From which our breath inhales it, draws it down
All through our bodies; sheep and cattle both
Succumb to such infections. Nor is there
One bit of difference whether we have gone
To places hostile to us, and have changed
Our old protective covering of sky,
Or whether nature, by some viciousness,
Inflicts on us infected atmosphere
Unusual, strange, and murderous.

                     Such a plague
Once visited Athens, blighted fields, laid waste
The highways, drained the town of citizens.
It rose from somewhere deep in Egypt, spread
Across long reaches of the skies and seas
Till finally it seized on all the folk
Of Pandion's town. They sickened and they died
In multitudes. At first they felt their heads
Burning with fever, and their eyes inflamed.
Throats blackened, sweating blood; and sores would block
The vocal passageways; the tongue, that tries
To be the mind's interpreter, filled up
Engorged with blood, became too hard to move,
Seemed rough to the touch. From throat to chest and lungs
The plague descended, thence assailed the heart,
Battering all the bastions of life.

The breath was horrible, reeking with a stench
Of carrion, the powers of mind would fail
With the weak body at the door of death.
The unendurable suffering increased,
Multiplied by the fret of anxiousness.
Groans and laments were mingled. Night and day
There was a constant retching, spasms clenched
Muscle and sinew, an exhausting drain
On the exhausted victims. You could not
Diagnose fever by the sense of touch
On bodily surfaces; they hardly seemed
More warm than normal, but a rash broke out
All over the body, pustulant and red
As erysipelas' fire. Men's inner parts
Were burning, burning to their very bones,
Their guts were furnaces. No man could bear
The lightest sort of coverlet; only air
Or a chill wind could bring relief. On fire,
They hurled their bodies, naked, into streams.
Many, with mouths wide-craving-open, plunged
Headfirst into deep wells, from any height.
The only thing they had to drink was thirst
Which drowned them utterly, made a deluge seem
Less than a raindrop. Weary bodies knew
No rest, no respite. Doctors shook their heads
And muttered in a silent fear, while patients
Stared blankly or kept rolling sleepless eyes.
The signs of death were obvious: the mind
Was crazed with grief and fear, the brow was knit,
Expressions fierce and wild, the ears would ring,
Breathing was labored or irregular,
Cold sweat would bead the neck, the spittle seemed
Stringy, pus-colored, salty, and a cough
Could hardly bring it up from the hoarse throat.
The hands would jerk, limbs tremble, and a chill
Crept up from the feet, a little at a time.
In the last stages, nostrils were compressed,
The eyes and temples hollow, and the skin

Both cold and hard, the forehead swollen tight,
The grin of rictus on the mouth. Eight days
Or nine would find the limbs grow stiff in death.
Some might survive a little longer; these
Found death still waiting, after stinking sores,
After black diarrhoea, or excess
Of hemorrhage from the nostrils. If a man
Survived even this, still the disease went on
Through joints and sinews, through the genitals,
And some men, in their dread of death, became
Self-surgeons, eunuchs, amputators—lost,
Blind victims of amnesia, gone from all
The selves they used to know. Cadavers lay
Piled up on others, but the dogs and vultures
Fled from the stench, or if they ever made
The slightest touch or taste, they would collapse
In sudden death. But under suns like those
Hardly a bird was ever seen, no beasts
Came from the forest; they were equally
Stricken and dying. First those friends of man,
The faithful dogs, succumbed on roads and streets.
There seemed to be no certain remedy,
No sound specific; what gave life to one
Killed others. The most pitiful thing of all
Was desperation, loss of nerve. A man
Finding himself laid low by the disease
Would lose all hope, would lie abject and stunned
Resigned to the death-sentence, with no thought
In mind save that, until he met his doom.
This plague was most infectious; it could spread
As pestilences do with animals,
Cattle and sheep. So death was piled on death.
Some people, when their kin were stricken, shunned
All visitation with them, but they paid
For their excessive appetite for life,
Their coward fear of death—their unconcern
Became a Nemesis, and laid them low,
Deserted, helpless, in ignoble death.

The loyal were no better off, worn out
By labors of devotion, by their own
Compelling sense of decency, by the voices
In which affection mingled with reproach.
So the most noble spirits perished. None
Were left, sometimes, as mourners, when the dead
Were hurried to their graves. Battles broke out
As the survivors fought for funeral pyres
With corpses heaped on corpses. Those who came
Back to their homes again were spent with grief,
Lying exhausted on their beds. Not one
Could possibly be found whom neither death,
Disease, nor mourning, at this frightful time,
Had left untouched.

                And out beyond the town
Shepherds and drovers and strong farmers lay
Huddled in their poor cabins. You could see
Dead parents with dead children for their pallets
Or children yielding up their little lives
On the bodies of dead parents. Country folk
Brought the disease to town, came streaming in
From areas of infection, filling all
The buildings and whatever open space
Might be available. Death piled them high
In crowded stacks. Beside the aqueducts
Lay many who had crawled or rolled as close
To the sweet water as their failing breath
Would let them manage. All along the streets,
In all the squares, you'd find the bodies, caked
With their own filth, rag-covered, or with skin
The only drapery across their bones
And that almost invisible under the crust
Of sores and ulcers. Even the shrines of the gods
Were charnel houses, and cadavers lay
Where guides had once conducted visitors.
The gods were paid no worship—no one thought
Their presence worth a straw—the state of grief

Had altered all proportion. Funeral rites,
Interments, which these pious people held
In all traditional reverence, became
Quite out of fashion; everyone in grief
Buried his own whatever way he could
Amid the general panic. Sudden need
And poverty persuaded men to use
Horrible makeshifts; howling, they would place
Their dead on pyres prepared for other men,
Apply the torches, maim and bleed and brawl
To keep the corpses from abandonment.

Synopses and Notes
(Numeration as in Loeb Classical Library)

BOOK I

Synopsis: Introduction: Invocation to Venus and appeal to the poet's patron, Memmius, 1-145; the two basic postulates of atomism, infinite atoms moving in infinite space or void, 146-447; everything else (e.g. time, historical events) is a property or accident of atoms and void, 448-482; the characteristics of atoms, 483-634; refutation of rival theories, 635-920; infinity of matter and space, 951-1117.

Notes

2. Venus is a symbol of the creative power of Nature and also a deity especially cultivated by the family of Memmius, the poet's patron (26).

66: "A man of Greece," i.e., the philosopher Epicurus, who wrote many technical works on atomic theory. One of his more popular treatises was extensively used by Lucretius in constructing the present poetic version of Epicureanism.

155. "Nothing can be created from nothing," the first principle of atomic materialism, has as its companion "nothing can be reduced to nothing" (216). Basic atomic matter is constant in quantity, uncreated and indestructible, in other words, eternal. The first principle has as its corollary, "all things are produced from fixed seeds" (206), i.e., by regular processes of natural causation, and not in a random or spontaneous manner. This deterministic corollary becomes a powerful weapon used by Lucretius in his warfare on superstition, religion, and popular belief in the arbitrary intervention of the gods in nature and human affairs.

371. "What some pretend," i.e., the rival school of the Stoics, who held that there is no empty space and that things move by exchanging places.

459. In Epicurean theory there are only two basic reals, matter in motion, and empty space. Time, therefore, contrary to what the Stoics maintained, is not a cosmic dimension or an independent entity, but only a sensation we get from bodies in motion or at rest. Events are aggregates of such

bodies localized in space, and historical events in the past, such as the Trojan War, are dependent "accidents" of the bodies and places involved.

599. Though the Lucretian atom is ultimate and indivisible, it nevertheless consists of a finite number of parts which are inseparable and have never come together to form the atom proper. To clarify this, Lucretius appeals to an empirical analogy: every perceptible body has an extreme point beyond which vision cannot go (e.g., the tip of a pin), but we can readily imagine that this point is made up of a number of tiny sub-points which are inseparable from the point itself. So it is with the atom, which consists of a number of "least parts" that are essential components of the atom proper but have never had and can never have separate existence. But the number of such ultimate particles is finite and probably small, because, as Lucretius points out, if each atom were infinitely subdivisible there would be no difference between the infinitely large and the infinitely small, i.e., the totality of things and the infinitesimal sub-particle. This reasoning, however, rests on the assumption that all infinities are equal, an obvious semantic error.

635. Heraclitus (ca. 510 B.C.), an early monist, held that the primary element, fire, exists as itself, yet successively changes into the other elements air, water, earth. All physical objects come into being through this "downward" flow of the elements from fire, but the dynamics of nature are such that they are simultaneously being disintegrated by an "upward" flow of the same elements, in reverse order, back to fire. Things owe their relative stability and identity to this dialectical tension of the two opposing "paths," but at the heart of nature there is only eternal flux in which "all things flow." Atomists like Lucretius did not object to the dynamic interpretation of nature, but to Heraclitus' assertion of the lack of absolute permanence and identity in the ultimate constituents of nature. That a single element, fire, is both itself and not itself at the same time is not only logically self-contradictory but metaphysically untenable: there must be durable and self-identical units of matter underlying the whole fabric of nature; otherwise things will be reduced to nothing and arise from nothing.

716. Empedocles (ca. 450 B.C.), a pluralist and one of the forerunners of the Atomists, held that there are four basic stuffs—earth, air, fire, water— each of which is eternal, unchanging, and infinitely divisible, and that physical objects are the product of these, in varying proportions, by mechanical combination. Lucretius' basic objections to this view are that four elements could not possibly account for the enormous variety of natural objects, and that incompatible stuffs such as water and fire must somehow have changed and lost their identity in the process of combining. But for a thing to become something it is not is self-contradictory and implies lack of permanence in the fundamental structure of matter.

830. Anaxagoras (ca. 440 B.C.) refined the pluralism of Empedocles by

postulating as many types of particles as there are natural qualities, instead of merely four elements. In this way he hoped to account for the diversity of physical things and to forestall the charge that any basic particle had changed or lost identity in combining with others. Thus bone is composed mainly of bone "seeds" or particles, blood of blood particles, hair of hair particles, and so on. In order to account for all cases of natural change from one state to another, he held also that "all things are in all things." Thus blood contains a preponderance of "seeds" of blood, but also a slight admixture of bone, hair, hot, cold, dry, and wet "seeds," etc. —in this way he aimed to explain why blood in one state is warm and fluid, in another cold and dry. Lucretius counters this *tour de force* by pointing out that Anaxagoras' elements are all too "weak" and impermanent to withstand destruction; and if basic particles can be reduced to nothing, there is nothing in theory to prevent things from arising from nothing, a natural impossibility.

1053. "As some say," i.e., the Stoics. The Epicureans, appealing to empirical analogy, held, on the contrary, that matter naturally "falls" downward through infinite space in which there is no top, no bottom, no middle. This concluding passage of Book I is a typical example of one of Lucretius' favorite techniques of rebuttal, the *reductio ad absurdum*. This consists in showing the irrational consequences of your opponent's position, thereby establishing negatively your own position by reducing his to absurdity.

BOOK II

Synopsis: Introduction: The good life, 1-61; the varieties of atomic motion, 62-215; the atomic swerve and its consequences, 216-293; the conservation of energy, 294-332; the variety of atomic shapes and the effects of these on sensation, 333-729; atoms have no secondary qualities such as color, temperature, etc., 730-1047; worlds are infinite and all mechanically formed like our own, 1048-1174.

Notes

18. Contrary to the popular stereotype, the Epicureans did not subscribe to the maxim of "Eat, drink, and make merry," but to a rather austere and negative hedonism: the good life is one which is as free as possible from bodily pains and mental distress or anxiety. To this end they recommended withdrawal from the competitive and acquisitive life, and extreme simplicity of living. They preferred to live not as individuals in society but in small communities of their own, such as the famous walled Garden of Epicurus in Athens.

114. Lucretius tells us that single atoms moving freely in space travel faster than light. When trapped in a compound body composed of millions of particles they continue to move at normal speed but their paths are foreshortened and deflected by constant collisions with neighboring atoms, so that the body as a whole is a mass of swirling and jostling particles. The cumulative effect of these internal collisions is to slow down the motion of the compound body, so much so sometimes that it becomes visible to the human eye, like the motes in the sunbeam.

167. The gods neither create nor maintain the physical universe. They are totally without desires or passions, either of love or hate, and are completely unaware of the existence of mankind. Their sole function is to serve as ethical models of spiritual calm and tranquility. In other words, the Epicureans dehumanized the ancient gods of Olympus to such an extent that they became faceless abstractions or, more accurately, ideal projections of what human beings should strive to become. In strict theory, the physical universe is "a fortuitous concourse of atoms," i.e., the undesigned and purposeless product of matter in motion; but the reader should note that in Lucretius Venus or Nature seems often to be the ghost of the old creator gods.

216. Free atoms falling through space in straight lines travel at equal velocities and in theory can never collide or coalesce into masses. Hence the notorious *ad hoc* hypothesis of the atomic swerve, which was designed by Epicurus to account for two entirely different things, both equally important. (1) The occasional swerving of atoms from the perpendicular (an element of pure chance in an otherwise deterministic system) makes possible collisions between atoms and also the cumulative massing of larger and larger aggregates, which eventually become entire worlds. Thus, according to Lucretius, the very existence of our world necessitates the postulation of the swerve. (2) Likewise, occasional swervings of atoms within the human soul make free will possible. If moral man were not free from the normal mechanisms, the atoms composing his soul would compel him to obey the iron laws of determinism and he would be a complete prisoner of matter and hence a moral automaton. Epicurus considered bondage to matter worse than the tyranny of willful and irrational gods; but our own feelings of freedom, Lucretius testifies, are evidence that we *are* free. But if man's freedom and moral responsibility rest on the random and unpredictable swervings of atoms, he is still the prisoner of these uncontrollable mechanisms and no better than a moral freak. Atomic behavior and moral freedom belong to entirely different orders of things and cannot be brought together in this way.

422. All physical bodies give off thin, hollow films from their surfaces, which are composed of the same types of atoms as the parent bodies, and have the same configurations. These on making contact with our sense

organs set up intricate patterns of atomic vibration which we experience as sensations, whether of sight, hearing, taste, smell, or touch. A sensation is pleasant or unpleasant, says Lucretius, depending on the various shapes of the incoming atoms, e.g., smooth and round as against hooked, barbed, and angular.

730. One of the great advances in theory made by atomism was the elimination of all sensory qualities from the atom and the consequent explanation of natural qualities in terms of quantity. No atom has color, temperature, taste, moisture, etc., and yet we perceive complexes of atoms (i.e., "things") as having color, temperature, taste, sound, and various tactile qualities. These experienced properties of things are the gross effects on our sense organs of the shapes, spatial arrangements, and velocities of the atomic complexes that stream into our senses from external objects. Thus by distinguishing the objective from the subjective—the quantitative aspects of nature from the qualitative aspects of experience—atomists like Democritus, Epicurus and Lucretius took a long step forward toward the scientific outlook.

740. Ordinarily the mind thinks in terms of the sensory images that it receives empirically, but it also has the power of "projecting itself" beyond experience and of thinking abstractions such as "atom" or "atom without color." Here the point is reinforced by an analogy: a blind person can recognize by touch an object whose color he cannot see; in the same way the mind can conceive of atoms as touchable but uncolored.

865. One of the most difficult problems facing a naive materialism such as that of Lucretius is to explain the phenomena of sensation, life, and mind. If no atom of itself has sensation or life or consciousness, how are we to explain the fact that certain atomic complexes such as man have all three of these properties? There can be no appeal, on principle, to divine creation (see note on 167 above). Lucretius' empirical examples (e.g., living worms emerging from dung heaps, various foods changing into living creatures, etc.) are not enlightening, nor will it do to appeal simply to the size, shape, arrangement, and motion of the constituent atoms. Clearly nature is not the arithmetical sum of its mechanical parts. Something new has been added; nature has created real entities not present at the most fundamental levels of matter. In the nineteenth and twentieth centuries more mature naturalistic theories proposed various types of emergent evolution: as the physical and chemical components of matter increased in complexity, various levels of thinking matter, sentient matter, and living matter gradually "emerged" by natural causation, each higher level presupposing the ones preceding it. But historically evolution still lay in the distant future, outside the theoretical scope of ancient atomism.

1047. The ideas of infinite space beyond our local world and of infinite worlds in that space are obviously not empirical in origin, but products of the mind's capacity to project itself beyond experience. See note on line 740 above.

BOOK III

Synopsis: Epicurus as therapist of the soul, 1-30; the fear of hell as the root cause of human vices, 31-93; material nature of mind and soul—their interrelations and their relation to the body, 94-416; various arguments for the mortality of the soul, 417-829; "Death is nothing to us," hell is man's present life, 830-1094.

Notes

3. "Glory of the Greek race," i.e., Epicurus. From this and other passages it is evident that Epicurus is no mere philosopher but in the two hundred years since his death has become, at least for Lucretius, a kind of cult figure, a healer of souls, and a revealer of absolute truths. With the decay of the Greek city states that followed Alexander the Great, the citizen felt spiritually uprooted, deprived of that civic framework which had previously given his life direction and meaning. To fill this void there arose two competing "salvation philosophies," Epicureanism and Stoicism, each of which offered their contemporaries a meaningful way of life together with a rational account of the world as a whole. In both cases the theoretical world view is designed to provide the essential groundwork for the therapy of dislocated and unhappy souls. The sick soul must first learn the nature of reality before it can take steps to lead the good life.

37. The fear of hell was one of the major social phobias that Epicureanism sought to neutralize by a rational appeal to atomic theory. In this interesting and quite typical passage Lucretius simplistically traces many of the outstanding human vices—ambition, envy, self-pity, murder, cruelty, etc. —to this single root cause. Men do evil because they are blindly trying to postpone the day of death.

94. It is essential for Lucretius to show the material character of the soul since he is about to launch into a series of arguments proving that it cannot survive death. The mind proper *(animus)* is made up of round, smooth, and very mobile atoms localized in the breast; it performs the functions of thinking and willing. The spirit *(anima)* is composed of similar "soul atoms" but is deployed throughout the body, where it interacts with coarser body atoms; its function is sensation. Mind and spirit may act separately or in unison; both act on the body by atomic contact and the body on them. In many contexts they are not distinguished but are referred to collectively as "the soul." The material nature of the soul, then, is a logically necessary part of a consistent system of thought, but it

was precisely this lack of "spirituality" and separate survival in the soul that made Epicureanism repellent to many, and accounted for its relative unpopularity.

371. Democritus (ca. 430 B.C.) was the philosophical predecessor of Epicurus and one of the two originators of the atomic theory.

417. The next four hundred lines are given over to more than twenty proofs of the standard Epicurean thesis that the soul is mortal and cannot possibly survive the breakup of the organic unity of body and soul. This literary *tour de force* is not necessarily traceable to the poet's morbid or pathological fascination with death (actually we know almost nothing about him and his personality), but is more likely an expression of the same didactic zeal that is evident in all parts of the poem. By demonstrating that the soul comes to a final and necessary end, Lucretius is preparing to convince his readers of an even more important point, that death is a mere word and not a possible experience, and that therefore the fear of death and the afterlife is absolutely groundless and irrational. If the convert to Epicureanism is to enjoy serenity and freedom from mental pain he must first rid himself of these two major phobias. As always, the good life presupposes rational acceptance of "the way things are."

The various arguments, which are of varying degrees of cogency, may be broken down into several general groupings: 1, proofs from the material makeup of the soul; 2, proofs from diseases (including psychosomatic ones) and their cures; 3, proofs from the parallelism of body and soul; and 4, proofs from the absurdity of supposing that the soul can exist separately.

800. Another example of the *reductio ad absurdum;* see note on Book I, 1053.

830. The two-hundred-line passage from this point on to the end of Book III is one of the most powerful in Lucretius and could indeed be considered as the climax of the entire poem. If anyone considers Epicureanism to be a frivolous, self-interested, and sterile way of life—and there have been many who thought so—he will find his error refuted here by this passionate display of concern for humanity and sense of social mission.

978. By demythologizing hell Lucretius strikes at the root of the vicious nonsense that has been fostered by religion in one form or another from time immemorial. And by showing that fools and knaves create their own psychological hell here and now, he provides himself with the opportunity of emphasizing the positive and more attractive aspects of Epicureanism: the serenity and spiritual peace that result from a rational acceptance of reality. Unfortunately, this opportunity is not fully exploited; instead the poet ends on a note of bitterness, world-weariness, and disgust for those who crave to live.

1025. Ancus Marcius, the legendary fourth king of Rome, is taken here as an archetypal figure of the great man who died.

1029. I.e., Xerxes the Persian.

BOOK IV

Synopsis: Introduction: The poet's task is to teach, 1-25; atomic images or films, their existence and nature, 26-216; all our sensations are caused by atomic images, 217-721; how we think, 722-822; miscellaneous topics, e.g., food, sleep and dreams, etc., 823-1036; handbook on sex, 1037-1287.

Notes

30. The ingenious theory of atomic images or films that are thrown off in unbroken series by all physical objects is the prescientific ancestor of our modern theories of light waves and sound waves. It is completely consistent with ancient atomic theory but is presented by Lucretius more as an incontestable truth than as a scientific hypothesis awaiting verification. Since atoms and their motions lie deep below the level of human perception, the Epicureans were unable, with the means at their disposal, to offer empirical proof of the existence of the images, but were forced to shore up the theory by crude common-sense analogies which can readily be observed, e.g., smoke rising from burning wood, snakes and cicadas casting their skins, etc. In any case, the theory was of major importance to them if they were to explain perception and knowledge. We can think and know only what has come to us by sensory experience. Hence, this being their assumption, Lucretius and other Epicureans take great pains to show that the senses always give us the truth about things and that they are infallible, although it is equally true that the mind often misinterprets sensory evidence. All seeing, hearing, smelling, etc., are really nothing but the physical impact of incoming images on the atoms of our sense organs, which in turn are excited to create replicas of outer objects. But the qualitative aspects of our experience (e.g., the redness of the apple, the sourness of the lemon) are *our* responses to the quantitative aspects of the atoms, their size, shape, velocity, and spatial arrangement.

462. It is one of the chief dogmas of Epicureanism that the testimony of the senses cannot be refuted by logic or reason; furthermore, the senses cannot refute themselves nor each other. What seems to be the actual state of affairs (i.e., "true") at a given moment, via a given channel of sensation, *is* the actual state of affairs. This extreme empiricism, so radically at odds with most Greek philosophy, makes it difficult to account for error: how can we be mistaken about things, as we obviously are on many occasions? (Lucretius has just devoted more than a hundred lines to such illusions of the eye.) Actually, the senses mechanically channel

in raw data from the outer world and are not themselves equipped to interpret reality for us. This function belongs to the mind, which alone is able to pass judgment or misjudgment on the sensory materials. Error, then, is "an opinion of the mind" and nothing inherent in the senses themselves.

Any extreme doctrine invites criticism and this one is no exception. We can use one of Lucretius' own examples to show that the infallibility of the senses is an ambiguous if not actually self-contradictory position. A square tower seen at a distance seems to be round. Which is it actually? Is error present here? A mile away the tower is seen to be round and so it is to the viewer, because the sharp edges of the tower image have been rubbed off in transit through the air! The observer's senses have told him the truth and there is no error, but as he gets closer to the tower he sees it to be square. Both sensory reports are therefore "true" and the tower is seen to be both square and not square, depending on where you are. In ambiguous cases like this the Epicureans advised inspection close up, to enable the mind to come to a clear-cut judgment about the situation. This is a noteworthy advance toward what we today call empirical verification.

The Epicureans' dogmatic stand on the infallibility of the senses is due partly to their materialistic physics and partly to their opposition to competing points of view, especially rationalism and skepticism. (1) The ancient rationalists (e.g., the Platonists) held that the mind is able by its own logical processes to arrive at "the really real" or metaphysical truth quite independently of sensory experience. They wrote off the evidence of the senses as superficial and erroneous, and consequently downgraded the natural world in favor of a world of transcendental archetypes. In the long history of Western thought they now appear as obstructers of scientific development and much more deeply in error than the Epicureans, for, as Lucretius points out, reason is not self-supporting but must rest on the solid base of the senses, and unless the senses are regarded as reliable the findings of reason will be unreliable. In addition, our entire practical life, in fact our physical safety from moment to moment, presupposes that the senses tell us the truth about the world. (2) The Skeptics of Epicurus' time took the negative view that the "irresistible impressions" of the senses are shared by both the wise and the foolish, that they contain in themselves no criterion of truth or falsity, and that the mind which bases itself on such impressions is unable to distinguish between reliable knowledge and unreliable. There can be no certainty in any area, whether theoretical or practical, and the best we can hope for is probability. Since experience and reason are equally untrustworthy, they concluded, we have no absolute knowledge about anything. This cautious position is caricatured by Lucretius as self-refuting, for if a person holds that he knows nothing, he contradicts himself when he asserts that he knows that he knows nothing.

What then is truth? For the rationalist truth does not refer to the actual world but to mental constructs of "pure reason," such as internally consistent systems of logic and mathematics. For the Epicurean empiricist, truth does refer to the physical world and is a product of the mind passing correct judgments on sensory materials. For the Skeptic truth is at best probability and at worst a mere sound signifying nothing real.

722. The next hundred lines describe how we think and dream, and it will be seen immediately that this section is one of the weakest and least satisfactory parts of atomic theory. All thinking is imagistic and takes place under the impact of incoming images, finer in texture than sensory images, which have bypassed the ordinary organs of perception and made direct contact with the mind atoms, where they generate counterparts of themselves. We can think of real existent objects such as lions and mountains and also of nonexistent creatures such as centaurs, half man and half horse, or Cerberus the three-headed hound of Hades, because in the latter case chance collisions of normal images have resulted in combinations that produce these bizarre effects. And when we dream, the mind is taking in whole series of such free-floating odds and ends that are miraculously left over from other times and places. Since space is crowded with images of all sorts, new and old, it would seem to follow that our consciousness would be flooded continually with a sea of incoming debris. But no, Lucretius says, the mind by its free volition can focus its attention on any image or series of images it wishes, allowing all others, which are flimsy in any case, to be blotted out of consciousness. But if our "free volition" is actually dependent on the random swervings of our mind particles, it would seem that the act of attention which saves us from mental chaos is a matter of pure chance (see note on Book II, line 216).

Numerous other objections can be raised. For example: (1) We may agree that occasionally our thinking is imagistic and that we internally "see" representations of things without benefit of vision, but it is quite plain that most of our mental activity is in terms of (coded?) meanings and their interconnections. What goes on when we read a printed page may serve as an illustration. The verbal symbols do not excite a train of images, as Lucretius' mechanistic account would have it, but a sequence or structure of meanings. (2) By no means all of our thinking has to do with concrete things, as Lucretius' theory would require. A great deal of it is concerned with general ideas or abstractions, such as population explosion, mankind, gross national product, atomism, and the like. Lucretius' pages are studded with abstractions taken from physics and metaphysics. How does he account for their origin? He doesn't, and it would be absurd to say that the idea of mankind comes to us in the same way as our ideas of individual persons in daily life, because no general entity such as mankind exists in nature. But conceivably such general ideas could be accounted for empirically as the telescoping of countless sensory impressions of similar particulars: our class concepts might be mental constructs created from our or others' experience of things that resemble each other. (3) Thinking by means of mathematical or logical symbols and the setting up of deductive sequences of connection between these is clearly not the result of external mechanical impacts but of subtle organizational powers within the mind itself. All this is quite beyond the scope of the atomists' theory of how we think.

795. An obscure passage which is much clearer in the translation than in the Latin original. It seems to mean that images are not at our arbitrary beck and call, but that, since such a multitude of them is constantly infiltrating the consciousness, the mind voluntarily selects the one or ones it wishes to "see" and allows the rest to fade out. Having focused its attention, the mind is able to "project" itself and recover in a split second the entire sequence of images that are telescoped in the first of the series.

823. An important point in mechanistic atomism. According to this point of view, known as anti-teleology, neither natural processes nor the universe as a whole exhibit purpose or design. To admit design into their world view would have been contradictory to the atomists' materialistic physics and their purely ethical theology (see Book II, note on line 167). Nature is a vast indifferent system of blind mechanical impulses which produces, by regular causal processes, a whole host of atomic aggregates such as organisms with their various organs of perception, etc. The fact that the eye sees is no indication of its having been designed by gods (or God) for the purpose of seeing; on the contrary, as Lucretius puts it, the eye, once created, later acquired its characteristic function. Since the main tradition of Greek philosophy, especially in the hands of Plato and Aristotle, was strongly in favor of world design or teleology, the contrary tendency in atomism was not only revolutionary but counted heavily against its popular acceptance. Nonetheless, the atomists now seem to be the children of light, since biological science, in fact science in general, has rejected the notion of teleology as theological and unscientific (i.e., incapable of being experimentally verified).

1037. The last 250 lines of Book IV have acquired a certain notoriety because they are a kind of handbook on sex composed by a philosophical poet, who presumably should never have gotten involved in such a topic. But sex plays a role in most of the Latin poets and Lucretius' treatment of it is relatively tame compared to that of some of his sexier confrères, Catullus, Juvenal, and Martial. In the first place, Lucretius' whole point of view is naturalistic and he is interested in explaining all things natural, so that it is not surprising that large portions of this section are straightforwardly informative and didactic, such as his accounts of the cause of physical desire, sex and diet, orgasm in women, heredity, incompatibility in marriage, positions in copulation, etc. Secondly, as a moralist intent on promoting the good life, he exhorts his readers to shun the disease of love, and savagely lampoons the grand passion: sex is more painful than pleasurable; it is frenzied and insatiable, a frightful composite of sadism and masochism; it wastes a man's bodily strength and leads to financial ruin; women are meretricious schemers who lay snares, all cats are alike in the dark, men in love are damn fools utterly bereft of reason. These stereotypes were already old in Lucretius' day. Critical judgments on this section of the poem have ranged from the squeamish and prudish to the clinical. One thing, however, is plain from the poem itself: Lucretius was a genuine Epicurean and as such it was quite normal for him to take a doctrinaire attitude toward sex and to denounce it as a pernicious evil destructive of higher values. Epicurus himself had written, "Sex never benefited anyone, and it is a marvel if it has not harmed him," and the whole moral trend of the school was toward minimizing pain in mind and body. What wonder then that the most turbulent of passions should be condemned as a natural foe of spiritual calm and serenity? We may well question Lucretius' scale of values but not his integrity as an Epicurean.

BOOK V

Synopsis: Epicurus, revealer of philosophical wisdom and moral healer, 1-54; the world is mortal, its origin was mechanical, not divine, 55-508; astronomical questions, 509-770; origin of vegetable, animal, and human life, 771-1010; early man in the state of nature, and the beginnings of civilization, 1011-1457.

Notes

9. It is obvious from this and similar passages that Epicureanism had by Lucretius' time become a substitute for conventional religion, and that Epicurus was now the spiritual healer who showed the convert how to imitate the ideal blessedness of the gods by the twofold therapy of moral catharsis and "revealed" knowledge. Philosophy—in this case, atomic theory—is able to cleanse man of his animal ignorance about the world and emancipate him from his childish dread of the supernatural; it can also "purify" his irrational desires by showing him that moral health means living a life governed by the natural mechanisms of pleasure and pain so as to achieve, not a maximum of pleasure, but a minimum of pain in body and mind. In this passage Epicurus is frankly held up as a god and given a status higher than that of the ancient culture-heroes, Ceres, Bacchus, and Hercules. The latter receives special attention only because he was a favorite of the despised Stoic school.

115. The heavenly bodies were widely regarded as divinities in Hellenistic times; but, as Lucretius shows, divinity implies the presence of mind and mind is not associated with any and every body, but only with human flesh and blood.

146. Ever since the time of Aristotle it was the fashion in Greek philosophy, except among the Stoics, to regard the gods (or God) as immobile and
self-contemplating; they expended no energy in either creating or main-
taining the universe but remained absorbed in their own perfection, unconcerned with the world and human beings. As far as the mechanics of
nature were concerned, Epicurus could readily have dispensed with gods
completely and candidly professed atheism. Instead, as a traditionalist, he
insisted on their existence but he dehumanized them and relegated them
to remote regions between the worlds, where they led lives of eternal calm
and bliss, serving as models for all committed Epicureans to imitate. Like
everything else in the world, the gods' bodies are atomic and radiate
images throughout infinite space, but their matter is very fine and attenu-
ated—in other words, practically "spiritual" but not quite incorporeal.

Some scholars have reasonably conjectured that Lucretius intended to
devote a final (seventh) Book to religion, theology, and ethics, instead of
closing the poem as he did on the unlikely topic of the plague in Athens,
but for some unknown reason (insanity? death?) he failed to do so.

235. Lucretius is arguing by empirical analogy from part to whole in a
kind of inductive extrapolation: since the component parts of the world—
earth, water, air, fire—are mortal, the world as a whole is mortal. In a
materialistic system such as this all compound bodies, large and small,
are subject to birth and death. Only the combining atoms are without beginning and end, i.e., eternal.

416. The marvelously imaginative passage that follows describes the original chaos of atoms that preceded the genesis of our local world, and
emphasizes once more the complete lack of design (ateleology) that
brought things to the state where they now are (see Book IV, note on line
823). The chance collision of billions of swirling atoms in the beginning resulted at first in unstable combinations, but these were gradually superseded by more "harmonious unions" of like with like, until finally the
major parts of the world—earth, water, air, and fiery ether—were separated
out mechanically from the original undifferentiated mass. By extrapolation
the atomists found it easy to postulate a similar origin for the millions of
other worlds that exist throughout space.

It is noteworthy here that Lucretius, like most Greco-Roman cosmolo-
gists, was the prisoner of the naive theory of the four elements and that
this theory apparently dictated the ancient geocentric model of the world
which he next describes. Earth, the heaviest of the elements, is suspended
at the center of a circular, rotating universe and is partially surrounded
by the next heaviest element, water. Then comes a wide band of air, a
relatively light element, which in turn is encased by the lightest of all
the elements, ether, which makes up "the flaming walls of the world";
in this move those fiery globules called stars. The spheres of sun and
moon rotate in the atmosphere between ether and earth, since they are

neither so heavy as to settle downward nor so light as to be borne aloft.

509. From this point on, and for the next 250 lines, Lucretius makes a systematic attempt to give a naturalistic account of various celestial phenomena and to avoid all mythological and teleological explanations. Since the phenomena of the sky were too remote for direct empirical observation and since ancient science was still at a primitive, non-experimental stage, the Epicureans were content to propose a variety of possible "causes" for a given phenomenon and to regard them all as equally plausible so long as none of them contradicted the evidence of the senses. Their criterion for the truth of a hypothesis, then, was its compatibility with common sense experience, rather than experimental verification by means of precision instruments, which of course were then non-existent. This method was essentially sterile and unproductive of scientific truth (except by accident), but at least it did produce a mass of fanciful theories, the accumulation, no doubt, of several centuries of speculation.

In the present passage, for example, four separate "causes" of the motion of the stars are proposed: (1) the stars move with the disk of the sky, in a body and not singly, and the sky is propelled by currents of air, either above it, or below it, or both; (2) the sky is stationary and the stars move singly, each driven by fiery ether that is trapped inside and seeks escape; (3) individual stars are propelled by random currents of air flowing in from outside; and (4) the stars move like sheep in pasture, each seeking its "food" in the fiery meadows of the ether. All of these "causes" of stellar motion are on a par in Lucretius' eyes and he makes no pretense to decide between them. The only test a theory must meet is that it shall not be inconsistent with some analogous situation in our sensory experience. For example, we could conceivably construct a hollow globe embossed with "stars," and by suspending it on an axis and blowing on it vigorously above and below make it revolve. Thus, theory (1) above, although not directly confirmed, is at least not contradicted by our experience.

564. The astounding information that sun, moon, and stars are approximately the same size as we see them represents a direct application of the Epicurean principle that the senses are infallible and their evidence is to be accepted without question (see Book IV, note on line 462).

622. Democritus was one of the two originators of the atomic theory in the fifth century B.C. The theory was almost four hundred years old by the time Lucretius wrote.

648. This curious hypothesis that the sun, moon, and stars are driven by alternating wind currents is aptly illustrated by the empirical analogy of cloud levels moving in opposite directions. The analogy does not confirm the hypothesis but simply shows that the latter is not contrary to our sensory experience.

680. The geocentric model of the world pictured a perfect sphere revolving on a tilted axis around a stationary earth at the center, and containing sun, moon, planets and fixed stars turning in their separate orbits. This globe is bisected by the equator, whose plane is equidistant from the two poles of the axis and perpendicular to it. The yearly circular path of the sun (or ecliptic) through the twelve signs of the zodiac (a narrow belt of sky on either side of the ecliptic) was set at an angle to the equator, and when the sun reached the rim on either the north or south side of the globe it was said to "turn back" in its orbit and move toward the other side of the world. The point of the sun's turning back was known in Greek as the *tropic*; thus, depending on the season, the sun was in the Tropic of Capricorn (winter, with the days consequently at their shortest) or in the Tropic of Cancer (summer, with longest periods of sunlight). The two points at which the sun's orbit cuts across the great circle of the equator are the equinoxes (spring and autumn), and here the periods of day and night are exactly equal all over the earth.

This model of the universe persisted for many centuries after Lucretius' time. It was provided with an elaborate mathematical base by the great astronomer Ptolemy of Alexandria (second century, A.D.), was further consolidated by the Roman Catholic Church in the Middle Ages for theological reasons (especially the centrality of man in the Creation), and was finally superseded, amid controversy, by the present heliocentric theory of Copernicus and Galileo in the sixteenth and seventeenth centuries.

762. This is of course the correct explanation of a lunar eclipse, but it is quite inconsistent with Lucretius' previous statement that sun and moon are approximately the same size as we see them. If this were the case, the shadow cast by a relatively large earth would be huge, not cone-shaped, and would envelop the moon for periods longer than normal.

837. This surrealistic picture of early life-forms points up the blind and random productive power of nature and is not an anticipation of evolution as we understand it today (the development of life from simple to increasingly complex forms). Once the existing species of plants and animals had established themselves and were able to survive and propagate, they remained permanently unchanged; they had no prehistory and no later development. Like other writers of his time, Lucretius accepts without criticism the standard doctrine of the fixity of species. Nevertheless, like others before him, he is clearly appealing to a principle of natural selection in this passage: only those species survived which had biological properties adequate to their environmental needs.

925. The famous account of early man and the beginnings of civilization that extends from this point for more than five hundred lines to the end of Book V is thoroughly realistic in tone, as would be expected from a writer like Lucretius. Although probably not based on any scientific an-

thropological evidence, it is certainly a more believable account than the romanticized descriptions of a legendary Golden Age, so current in the poetic literature of antiquity. It is flawed here and there by moralizing, when the poet contrasts the austerity of primitive times with the spreading corruption of his own era.

1019. This point in human history marked the informal beginnings of a social compact "not to harm or be harmed," which was later reinforced by the conscious and voluntary submission of the people to the rule of law (lines 1145 ff.). In thus providing for his own greater security and chances for survival, primitive man was intuitively obeying the pleasure/pain principle, for, as it turned out, the best life for the community was one which minimized the social damage done by murder, theft, pillage, arson, etc. Epicurus himself had defined the concept of justice in much the same language: "Justice is a kind of agreement not to harm or be harmed, made when men associate with each other at any time and in communities of any size whatsoever."

1028. It was a moot question in antiquity whether language originated naturally or by convention, i.e., by deliberate rational invention. Epicurus had settled the matter by a compromise. The various racial groups at first evolved their own languages spontaneously. These primitive tongues were the physiological expressions of their differing emotional reactions to differing physical environments. Later on, reason came into play in the form of linguistic conventions which served to standardize both the structure of languages and the meanings of words, thereby facilitating communication within a given group and with other racial groups.

1161. Lucretius' account of the origin of religion is weak and unconvincing but consistent with the theory of atomic images which he described in Book IV (see note on line 30). The Epicureans had a marked contempt for all forms of popular religion because it debased the purity and majesty of the gods as they conceived them, since it rested on a vulgar contractual basis of "something for something" and encouraged feelings of fear and anxiety that destroyed the spiritual poise and calm they most desired; and its social effects throughout history had been generally evil. As a moral substitute they offered an attitude of natural piety toward the vast impersonal system of nature, a sophisticated state of mind that was to be attained only with the help of atomic theory and the philosophical contemplation of the nature of things as they really are. "True religion is the power of contemplating the whole with a spirit in repose." Despite these advanced views, Epicurus instructed his followers to observe scrupulously all the public rites and ceremonies of established religion; his motives in so doing are unclear.

1234. A bundle of rods surmounted by an axe (formerly represented on the back of the older issues of the U.S. dime) was the public symbol of the Roman magistrates' power to flog and execute.

1302. "Lucanian herds," i.e., armored elephants, used in Italy by Hannibal and the Carthaginian armies.

BOOK VI

Synopsis: Epicurus and the gods, 1-95; meteorology: thunder, lightning, waterspouts, etc., 96-534; miscellaneous earth phenomena: earthquakes, volcanoes, the magnet, etc., 535-1089; disease and plague, especially the great plague at Athens, 1090-1286.

Notes

5. Lucretius' final paean of praise to his master Epicurus, the moral savior of mankind and source of all truth.

50. For the Epicurean conception of the gods, see Book V, note on line 146. For a person to believe simultaneously that the gods are perfect, absolutely remote from man, unconcerned and totally immobile, and yet that they are in active control of all natural events such as the weather, is at the very least self-contradictory; more important, it debases their majesty to involve them in nature and undermines the spiritual calm of the worshipper if he approaches them in a fearful, anxious, or propitiatory state of mind. The gods do not punish any more than they reward or answer prayer. Nature and deity have nothing to do with each other: the one is a mechanical and self-regulating system, the other a Utopian state of being quite apart.

Since the Epicureans had a strong sense of social mission, their campaign against old-time superstition and the remnants of traditional anthropomorphic religion took the form of education in scientific principles, particularly the principle of causation. The most awe-inspiring events in nature—tempests, volcanic eruptions, thunder and lightning, earthquakes, plagues—are not the work of angry gods but of natural causes, nothing more or less, and it is to these that Lucretius now directs the reader's attention for the next twelve hundred lines of the poem.

96. In dealing with weather phenomena the Epicureans went to fantastic lengths in listing possible natural causes; here, for example, Lucretius sets down nine separate explanations of thunder, and later, four for lightning, four for thunderbolts, three for earthquakes, and so on. The reason for this piling up of theories was obviously to impress the ancient reader that these phenomena were simply the effects of natural causes and nothing more. Old religious habits of explanation had to be overlaid by a mass of evidence that was consistent with atomic theory and common sense. If the modern reader is put off or irritated by all this pseudo-scientific lore, he should remember that ancient science was still primitive and largely speculative and that it had no means at its disposal for verifying and falsify-

ing hypotheses. The naturalistic spirit may have been strong, but all the exact techniques that we associate with science still lay far in the future (see note on Book V, line 509).

160. Of the four elements Lucretius relies most heavily on fire and wind, either singly or in combination, in his meteorological explanations. Electricity was not understood until the eighteenth century, with Galvani, Volta, Franklin.

219. Lucretius devotes two hundred lines to the thunderbolt alone. His motives were partly scientific, but largely anti-religious, since the thunderbolt for centuries had been regarded as the special weapon of the chief god, Zeus, or Jupiter.

542. *"Things are like themselves,"* i.e., nature is uniform and what can happen on the surface of the earth can also happen below. The modern theory of earthquakes by geological faulting and slipping of rock strata sideways or up and down is a product of nineteenth century science. The wind theory developed by Lucretius in the next section had a long life and was used as late as 1755 to explain the great earthquake at Lisbon which took eighteen thousand lives.

647. In this section Lucretius is trying to answer the hostile objections of critics who had apparently pointed out that the Epicureans were using the same four elements time after time to explain a wide variety of natural phenomena, ranging from disease to the fires of Mt. Etna, that were totally different from each other in kind. Lucretius' reply is that the relatively tiny earth is constantly being supplied from the infinite reservoirs of the universe with more than enough materials to account for anything and everything that occurs here on our planet. But mere quantity of materials is not enough to account for the enormous qualitative differences in natural happenings. The passage demonstrates clearly how science is crippled when it is tied to inherited dogmas. The doctrine of the four elements was bankrupt centuries before Lucretius' time, and by continuing to appeal to it blindly and uncritically the Epicureans simply prolonged the infancy of science.

735. The Blue Nile rises in Lake Tana in Ethiopia; at Khartoum it is joined by the White Nile which rises far to the south in Lake Victoria. The geographer Ptolemy (ca. 150 A.D.) held that the (White) Nile rose from two great lakes south of the equator near a range of mountains he called the Mountains of the Moon (Ruwenzori); his information was approximately correct.

998. Lucretius' explanation of magnetism is an ingenious *tour de force:* all objects are constantly throwing off atoms from their outer surfaces. The loadstone or magnet, in giving off a heavy discharge of particles, evacuates the air between itself and the iron ring nearby. Into this vacuum particles from the ring immediately move, and since the atoms making up iron are very closely intertwined, the entire ring follows the leading parti-

cles until it makes contact with the loadstone. This extraordinary process is also assisted by the pressure of air within and behind the ring, which pushes it forward into the vacuum. The relationship between magnetism and electricity was not discovered until the early nineteenth century.

1138. In this spectacular account of the bubonic plague at Athens in 430 B.C. Lucretius closely followed the narrative of the Athenian historian Thucydides, who was an eyewitness.